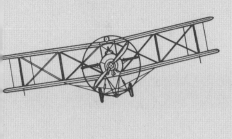
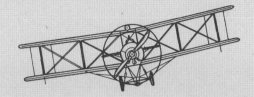
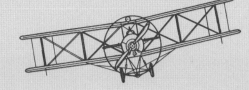
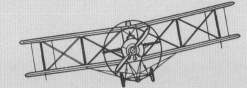

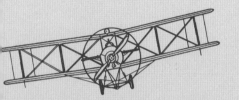

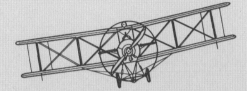
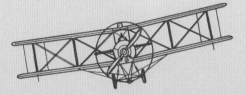

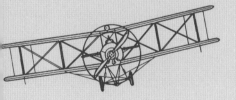
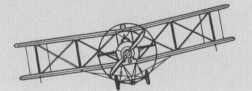
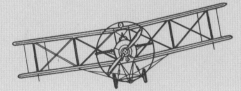

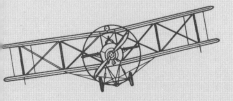
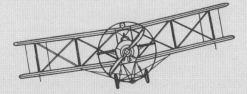
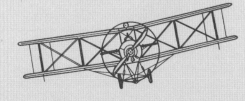
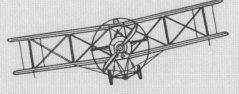

Pioneers of
AVIATION

Pioneers of
AVIATION

Christopher Chant

BARNES
&NOBLE
BOOKS
NEW YORK

Copyright © 2001 Regency House Publishing Limited.

2001 Barnes and Noble Books

M 10 9 8 7 6 5 4 3 2 1

ISBN 0-7607-2499-7

Printed in Hong Kong

PAGE 2
Irishman Professor George Francis Fitzgerald attempts to fly at College Park, Dublin in 1895, using towed gliders.

TITLE PAGE
Alberto Santos Dumont's No. 14-bis.

RIGHT
Henry Farman, an early pioneer.

Chapter One

The Triumph of the Wright Brothers

Successful flight in a heavier-than-air machine began with the first of four efforts made by the brothers Orville and Wilbur Wright on 17 December 1903. Indeed, there can be no doubt that this quartet of flights marked the start of the age of practical aviation, though they were also the culmination of the previous century's pioneering efforts. So the work of earlier pioneers, some of them realists and others of them simply dreamers, should not be discounted.

It was only after four years of experimental work with gliders that the Wright brothers were finally ready with their initial powered heavier-than-air craft, which was a machine driven by an engine they themselves had designed and built. The *Flyer I*, as this first real aeroplane is now known, was crated for transport from the Wright establishment in Dayton, Ohio to the Kill Devil Hills in North Carolina, where the machine was reassembled in December 1903. Although it is often claimed that the Wrights chose this location to ensure secrecy, the brothers really selected this deserted spot for its steady and moderately strong prevailing winds, which had greatly aided the brothers' gliding experiments in previous years.

The first attempt at a powered flight

designing and building a new machine that incorporated the lessons learned in North Carolina with the *Flyer I*.

The Wrights were the first men to fly successfully, but this should not be allowed to disguise the fact that men had indeed flown before. A succinct and generally satisfactory theory of flight's aerodynamic aspects had been evolved just over 100 years earlier by an Englishman, Sir George Cayley. In 1799 he had defined his theory concerning the forces acting on a body in flight and inscribed it on a silver disc. On the other side of the disc was a simple drawing of a glider containing all the elements necessary for flight. Cayley continued to work on the notion intermittently for the next 50 years before building a full-scale model in 1849. The control surfaces had to be fixed before flight, but several short glides were made with the machine in ballast before Cayley was ready to experiment with a live passenger in the form of the son of a worker from his estate near Scarborough. Although he was only a passenger, the unknown boy has the distinction of being the first person to fly in a heavier-than-air machine. Cayley continued to work on his designs and in 1853 produced an improved design, and in this his coachman was launched across a small valley on the estate. Cayley worked on the theory of flight until 1855.

Much greater things might have been expected from Cayley if an adequate power source had been available at the time. Cayley did experiment with various types of engine, but none of these proved successful, and Cayley was therefore limited to theory and gliding flight. This same factor bedevilled pioneers for the next quarter-century until the German

OPPOSITE
The Wright Flyer I *is seen at Kill Devil Hills, Kitty Hawk, North Carolina on 14 December 1903 after the Wright brothers' unsuccessful first attempt to take off in their first powered aeroplane. The forward corners of the booms carrying the front elevator assembly are dug into the sand, and Wilbur Wright is at the controls.*

ABOVE
Launch of the Wright Glider No. 3 in 1902 (in revised form with a single rather than twin rudder assembly) with Orville Wright at the controls. The glider helped the brothers to perfect their aerodynamic and structural thinking, and also to learn the rudiments of their piloting skills.

was made by Wilbur on 14 December, but the flight was unsuccessful when coarse movement of the control for the forward-mounted elevator sent the *Flyer* into the sand as it left its take-off trolley. Repairs were completed during the following days, and on 17 December the brothers were once again ready to continue their trials. After five local witnesses had arrived, Orville took his place prone on the lower wing of the *Flyer*, opened up the engine and signalled for the machine to be released. The *Flyer* gathered speed down the 60-ft (18-m) launching rail that had been laid into the wind and, as it reached its flying speed of about 25mph (40km/h), lifted off the trolley and entered wingborne flight. Twelve seconds later the *Flyer* touched down after covering about 500ft (150m)

through the air. The time was shortly after 10.35 a.m. During the next 90 minutes, three more flights were made, the last of them by Wilbur. This proved the most successful flight of the day, and covered more than 880yards (800m) in a time of 59 seconds.

The Wrights thus became the first men to fly a heavier-than-air machine that could take off from level ground, travel through the air under its own power, be effectively controlled during its flight in all three planes, and land at an altitude as high as that from which it had taken off.

The day's historic nature was reported to the press, but received little coverage and was largely ignored. Without any fuss, however, the Wrights then disassembled the *Flyer* and transported it back to Dayton, where they set about

ABOVE
Seen at the Kill Devil Hills in 1901, this is Wright's Glider No. 2 with a single forward elevator but no rear rudder.

RIGHT
This side view of the Wright Flyer I at the Kill Devil Hills in December 1903 reveals the aircraft's salient features including the very thin aerofoil section, the location of the opposite-turning propellers, the biplane forward elevator and rear rudder assemblies, and the skid landing gear.

N.A. Otto perfected his four-stroke internal combustion engine. There followed a short phase in which the petrol engine was developed in both power and reliability, but the pioneers of flight had to wait nearly another 25 years before engine technology reached the point at which it was possible to make a powerplant offering the power/weight ratio required for the petrol engine's use in an aeroplane.

The pioneers of flight were not entirely daunted by the lack of an effective engine, though, and the drawing boards of the pioneers were littered with a host of designs characterized by varying levels of practicality and safety. Many of these machines in fact reached the hardware stage: some were built as gliders, but most of them were constructed as powered machines with a great deal of faith pinned on gas, steam or even gunpowder engines.

One of the earliest of these pioneers was a Frenchman, Félix du Temple. In 1857 he produced his first successful powered model aeroplane, and in the same year designed a full-sized monoplane which was not in the event built until 1874, when it became the first powered aeroplane to take off after it had plunged down a steep ramp. The aeroplane was wholly incapable of sustained flight, however, and came down almost immediately after its launch. Some 16 years later, in 1890, the first take-off from level ground was made by another French aeroplane, the *Éole* designed by Clément Ader. This was a truly extraordinary machine configured something like a bat, with a fuselage-mounted steam engine driving a large tractor propeller. The machine took off and moved some 160ft (50m) through the air on 9 October 1890, but this can in no way be considered a true flight as the *Éole* lacked any type of control surface and was anyway incapable of sustained flight. Even so, Ader was highly encouraged by his success and pressed ahead with his experiments in heavier-than-air flight with similarly configured machines.

Cayley had first developed the theory of lift through the use of cambered wing surfaces, but almost 100 years intervened before Horatio Phillips, the first great aerodynamicist, patented his theory of lift based on a differential camber between the upper and lower surfaces of the wing section. If the curvature of the upper surface of a wing is greater than that of its under surface, according to this concept, the air flows over the upper surface at a greater velocity, resulting in a pressure lower than that on the underside of the wing. Hence an upward force, lift, is generated as the higher pressure under the surface seeks to equalize the pressure differential with the lower-pressure air above the surface. His first patent was granted in 1884, and less than ten years later, in an effort to prove his theories, Phillips made and flew a large multiplane model whose wing cellule of superimposed wings of very high aspect ratio resembled nothing so much as a venetian blind. However, Phillips' work was to prove invaluable to all future aircraft pioneers, for this far-sighted Englishman had paved the way to the future by his evolution of the theory of true aerodynamic lift in place of the planing lift used in kites and earlier powered aircraft efforts.

Though at times much has been claimed for the huge flying machine built in 1894 by Hiram Maxim, better known as the inventor of the first truly successful machine-gun, in reality little can be said for it. At vast expense, Maxim built a large biplane test rig to investigate the nature of lift. The test rig ran on a two-rail track, and was prevented from rising more than a few inches by wooden guard rails. During the course of a test run in 1894 the steam-powered machine produced enough lift to rise from its supporting track and even to break through the guard rails. It then crashed, as there were no means of controlling the machine in the air. Maxim thereupon abandoned his efforts, but later attempted to secure some of the glory awarded aviation pioneers by launching extravagant claims for his rig.

In 1897 Ader produced the *Avion III* as his third full-sized machine. This was similar in configuration to the *Éole*, but had two steam engines each driving its own propeller. Again, there was no adequate provision for controlling the machine in the event that it left the ground, which it did not. Nevertheless, claims for Ader to be considered the first man to fly have been made at various times since the beginning of the century.

All was not in vain during the last decade of the 19th century, however, for in another flight-related field great progress was being made. This was in the realm of gliding flight. Realizing that the absence of an engine with a suitable high power/weight ratio meant almost certain failure to the pioneers concentrating on flight by means of thrust and lift, more practically minded pioneers saw that gliding flight, in which the pull of gravity replaces the thrust of the propeller as the primary motive force, offered the chance of making real advances. Chief among these exponents of gliding was Otto Lilienthal, the great German pioneer. A practical man who believed in the scientific method, Lilienthal was content to advance by slow steps and therefore did not attempt to launch anything into the air until he had fully considered all aspects of the device. In common with many other pioneers, Lilienthal was fascinated by bird flight, but unlike most of his contemporaries he did not attempt to produce mechanical copies of birds. Instead he analyzed how birds fly and then sought to apply the same principles to a structure that was mechanically adequate to the demands placed on it. In 1889 Lilienthal published his findings on bird flight in *Der Vogelflug als Grundlage der Fliegerkunst*, a book that soon became the bible of future pioneers.

Lilienthal built his first glider in 1891, and by 1894 had developed the monoplane standard glider that proved highly successful and appeared in so many photographs of the period. Lilienthal's gliders were not without their faults, however: his concentration on aerofoils of parallel, rather than differential, camber was a step in the wrong direction after the tests carried out by Phillips, and his control system was adequate for his small gliders but could not be applied on anything else. Nevertheless, the important fact about Lilienthal's gliders was their success rather than their concept. Operating from his artificial mound in Berlin or from hilltops elsewhere in Germany, Lilienthal and his gliders proved that heavier-than-air flight, albeit of a not very practical form, was possible. This did much to increase a general enthusiasm for flight and also encouraged other pioneers to persevere in their endeavours despite their difficulties.

Lilienthal's control system was based on the movement of the glider's centre of gravity, rather than on the operation of control surfaces, in the manner later copied for modern hang-gliders. This system was made necessary by the lightweight and relatively flimsy structure of Lilienthal's machines, which could not easily have been made to incorporate moving surfaces and their controlling cables. The pilot was instead suspended by his upper chest in a gap between the wings, so that his legs could swing anywhere in the hemisphere below him. The lower half of his body and his legs were then moved in the direction he wished his craft to go, the movement of the centre of gravity in that direction effecting the change. This system also removed the need for landing gear, as the pilot merely ran down his chosen slope until he had reached flying speed and lifted off; landing was simply effected by touching down onto his feet.

Lilienthal went off at a tangent in 1896 when he began to experiment with ornithoptering (flapping) wings powered by a small gas engine. There is every reason to expect that he would have reverted to more practical forms of propulsion, but on 9 August 1896 Lilienthal stalled during a flight, crashed and died in hospital on the following day. Although Lilienthal was not always on the right track, his importance in the history of flight cannot be denied: he was both the first man to fly in a controllable aeroplane and the source of inspiration for the next generation of pioneers who were the men who would make powered flight a reality. From his time onwards the need for the effective means of controlling an aeroplane in the air was there for all to see. Earlier pioneers had not realized how important this factor

really was, imagining perhaps that the aeroplane would somehow fly and control itself once it had risen into the air.

Lilienthal's greatness may also be gauged from the spate of imitators he inspired, principally in the UK and USA. Percy Pilcher, a Scotsman, built the sturdy and practical *Hawk*, which had landing gear and could be towed off the ground, but this machine was still controlled in the Lilienthal hang-glider fashion. Pilcher's death after a gliding accident in 1899 was a great blow to the development of British aviation, for with his demise serious experimentation came to an end for nearly 10 years. In the USA

Lilienthal's imitators included Octave Chanute and A.M. Herring, the latter co-operating with Chanute in the design process and then doing most of the flying, since Chanute was too old for this onerous task. The two built a few relatively successful types in 1896 and 1897, but Chanute's real importance was as a propagandist of flight. Realizing that he was too old to contribute anything but ideas to the cause, he concentrated on helping and encouraging other younger and more dynamic designers, including the Wright brothers. Chanute did, however, improve upon the structural concept of the basic Lilienthal hang-glider

design by introducing the braced biplane formula, with its wing bays or cellules.

Similar progress in structures and aerodynamics was also being made at the same time by the Australian Lawrence Hargrave, who invented the box-kite in 1893. This type of flying toy gained considerable popularity in Europe and the USA in the late 1890s, and its basic shape was soon to be copied in a number of European aircraft, notably the Voisin and Farman types.

It is at this point that the Wright brothers enter the scene as Chanute's ablest students. Determined and serious, but each characterized by a high degree

of analytical and constructive imagination, the brothers belonged to a large, tight-knit family. Wilbur and Orville were the Wrights' third and fourth sons respectively, and in addition to two older brothers had a younger sister. From childhood, the two youngest brothers displayed the energy and enthusiasm that would eventually prove profitable. Wilbur and Orville, with the latter very much the driving spirit of the team, joined forces with a friend to start a weekly newspaper. The *West Side News* was undertaken in its entirety by the three young men, including the printing on a press built by Orville and Wilbur, then 18 and 22 years old respectively. In 1890 the three moved into a more ambitious project, *The Evening Item*, but this lasted for only four months before competition with the more securely established Dayton dailies forced them out of business.

But at this time a new type of bicycle, the safety bicycle with two equal-size wheels instead of one large and one small, was becoming popular and in this fact the brothers saw a good market for

their undoubted engineering skills. Setting up business at first to sell bicycles, they soon expanded to the repair of damaged machines and finally the manufacture of their own *Wright Special*. This retailed for the remarkably low price of $18 compared with the $160 Orville had paid for his first bicycle in 1892. The success of their bicycle business meant that the brothers had a secure, steady income and access to light engineering

equipment and facilities. Moreover, their work with bicycles gave them an early appreciation of the value in mechanical structures of lightness combined with strength, and also a keen insight into the closely allied factors of balance and control.

The brothers had been interested in flight from their youth when their father, the local bishop of the United Brethren Church, gave them a toy helicopter operated by a rubber band. Orville and Wilbur built replicas of the model, which flew successfully but met with failure when they tried to produce scaled-up examples: after several such failures they abandoned the idea. Over the next few years, the brothers' interest in flight was limited to an appreciation of birds' soaring flight.

Wilbur later revealed that his active interest in flight was spurred by the death of Lilienthal in 1896. Orville also underwent a renewal of enthusiasm, and the two decided to evolve and build a heavier-than-air flying machine. It was the nature of the brothers, however, not to rush into a subject about which they knew next to nothing, so Orville and Wilbur set about their task with a planned method. The brothers started by reading all that they could obtain, but took nothing as certain unless they had been able to verify it in their own experiments or through observation of soaring birds. From the first, the Wrights realized that the problem of flight was not how to get into the air, as this had been established by aviators such as Lilienthal and Chanute, and also by the engineers who were now producing more effective petrol engines. From the beginning, therefore, the brothers saw that the real problem lay in controlling

the aeroplane once it had risen into the air. Control in pitch around the lateral axis was simple as it demanded only a horizontal rudder: now known as the elevator, this could be mounted in front of or behind the wings. A vertical rudder, too, could cope with any yawing motion round the vertical axis. But the problem of control in roll around the longitudinal axis was more difficult. Lilienthal had been experimenting with controlled wing warping in which the wings could be twisted differentially so that the wing with its trailing edge forced down produced more lift than the other wing, with its trailing edge lifted up. The resulting differences in lift would roll the aeroplane toward the side with the lifted trailing edge, so giving a measure of control. But Lilienthal had failed to see that this mechanism produced further problems: the wing with the better lift would also have more drag, and so would slew the aeroplane round in yaw once the warping was applied.

From their observation of the flight of buzzards, the Wright brothers made the same discovery of the effects of differential warping of the wing tips, and in 1899 they decided to apply the same principle to their aeroplane. After establishing how their machine could be controlled in all three planes, the brothers then decided to make a practical beginning by constructiing a model kite-glider to test the wing warping. This first kite-glider spanned 5ft (1.52m), and was ready for testing in August 1899. In it structural features the kite-glider was related to Chanute's biplane glider, and had a fixed tailplane for longitudinal stability. Control was effected by four lines, and the kite proved very successful, the wing warping in particular producing a very impressive

performance. The wings had also been designed to move backward or forward in relation to each other to alter the centre of pressure, but this feature was not very useful and the brothers abandoned it in later models.

The Wrights' next step was clearly to build a small man-carrying glider, and this was ready by the autumn of 1900. It was similar to the 1899 kite-glider, but had a span of 17ft (5.18m) and the elevator was

located forward of the wing cellule as the Wrights thought that this would provide a control surface that would act more rapidly and therefore more effectively. The glider lacked any fixed horizontal surfaces allied to the elevator, and had no rudder.

The Wrights selected Kitty Hawk for the tests of their new machine as there were strong, steady winds there for most of the year, and because the sand of this coastal area would help mitigate the

Evident in this photograph of the Flyer I *just above the ground is the crossed nature of the chain drive to the port propeller and the asymmetric positioning of the pilot and engine on the lower wing.*

damaging effect of any heavy landings. Tests soon revealed that the wing area of the glider was insufficient to support the weight of a man unless the wind was quite strong. The glider was then flown mostly as a kite, when its success showed that the brothers were on the right lines. This No. 1 Glider was also tested with dihedral (an angle between the wing and an imaginary horizontal so that the wing tips are higher than the wing roots). This was meant as an aid to stability, but was found to make control so difficult in the strong breezes of Kitty Hawk that the Wrights abandoned the idea almost entirely. Indeed, they went to the opposite extreme of making their machines inherently unstable by giving the wings anhedral, so that the wing tips were lower than the wing roots.

Proceeding carefully, the brothers built their No. 2 Glider for further tests in 1901. Though it was similar to the No. 1 Glider in basic concept, the No. 2 Glider had its wing increased in span to 22ft (6.71m) so that its larger wing area would generate sufficient lift to carry a man aloft. Anhedral was again used, and a new warping mechanism was introduced: this latter comprised a cradle for the pilot's hips, so that when he swung his torso to the right or left as he lay on the lower wing, the wires attached to the cradle operated the warping mechanism. The new glider, flown over the Kill Devil Hills south of Kitty Hawk, proved only moderately successful, and the Wrights realized that there was still something wrong with their design.

The brothers decided that their lack of greater success indicated two major problems. Up to this point they had ignored their own strictures on the need for their own proofs and thus tended to take the figures in Lilienthal's book as gospel, but the tests of the No. 2 Glider now revealed that Lilienthal had favoured too pronounced a camber for the wing section. The Wrights therefore constructed a small wind tunnel, presumably the first ever built, and during the winter of 1901–2 undertook trials to correct Lilienthal's figures in the light of their own experience with gliders. The other problem was that of the slewing moment imparted to the glider when the wing warping mechanism was used. The Wright's first solution to this difficulty was the provision of a fixed double fin mounted on booms behind the wings to serve, the brothers hoped, as a stabilizing element and so correct any tendency for the aeroplane to turn toward the side of the positively warped wing.

Tests with the No. 3 Glider in September 1902 showed that far from solving the problem, this in fact worsened matters as once the slewing motion started, the aeroplane's tendency to side-slip, as a result of the banking, in fact caused the fins to act as a lever aiding the slewing moment. Orville and Wilbur rapidly appreciated the nature of the problem, and replaced the original fixed double fins with a single moving rudder. The control wires for this were fixed to the warp cradle so that when, for instance, right bank was applied the rudder moved automatically to the right to counteract any tendency for the machine to slew to the left. With this No. 3 Glider (Modified), which was flown during October 1902, the Wright brothers had finally developed their ideas into a fully practical gliding aeroplane that could be controlled in all three planes, and this was the basis of their future success.

The Wrights devoted the winter of 1902–3 to the building of their first powered aeroplane. The initial problem to be faced was the nature and disposition of the powerplant. The decision went in favour of two pusher propellers driven from a single engine by means of chain drives, one of them crossed so that the propellers rotated in opposite directions so that the torque of each propeller cancelled that of the other. The pilot would lie slightly to the left of the centreline with the engine marginally to the right so that the two weights would balance each other. The brothers soon realized that, as with virtually every component needed for their aircraft, they would have to make their own engine and propellers, there being no suitable units available on the commercial market. The propellers were efficient to a degree unmatched by other propellers for another six years, and the engine was an ingenious, light, but robust four-cylinder unit, which delivered 12hp (8.9kW) for a weight of 179lb (81.4kg).

The aeroplane specially built for the attempt at powered flight was similar to its predecessors in layout but somewhat larger, with a span of 40ft 4in (12.3m), 8ft 3in (2.5m) greater than that of the No. 3 Glider. To take advantage of their greater efficiency at lower speeds the propellers were geared down from the engine, and to avoid unnecessary complication and weight, landing gear of the skid rather than wheeled type was used. This landing gear posed problems of its own, however, as a special take-off technique had to be evolved. This involved the use of a 60-ft (18.3-m) grooved wooden rail on which ran a light wheeled trolley. The aeroplane rested on the trolley and was restrained by a tethering rope while the engine was run up to full power. Once the engine had reached full power, the rope was released and the trolley-mounted aeroplane accelerated along the rail until it reached flying speed and lifted into the air. It is worth noting that detractors of the Wrights' achievement have often claimed that the brothers did not succeed in making a powered, sustained flight in 1903 because they used an accelerating device to catapult the aeroplane into the air. This was not so: it was not until 1904 that the Wrights introduced their accelerator device, and then it served only as a refinement and not as an essential component of launching.

The Wrights took their *Flyer I* to Kill Devil Hills in December 1903. After rehearsing their techniques on a glider, on 17 December they made the first powered, sustained and controlled flights as they took off from level ground, climbed and then descended to ground no lower than that from which they had taken off. Although the day's events were reported in the press, this momentous occasion passed almost unremarked by the public. Orville and Wilbur Wright returned to Dayton to plan their next moves. Clearly the most important matter was to improve their aeroplane and its engine, for the combination had only just been able to fly. During the winter of 1903–4, therefore, the brothers built a new aeroplane almost identical to the *Flyer I* but with reduced camber. A new engine was also built, and this could deliver an extra 4hp (3kW).

Although not the furtive, secretive men they are sometimes labelled, the Wright brothers realized the commercial implications of their invention, and decided that their financial interests would be harmed by too much publicity before their patents had been fully secured. They therefore decided to operate their aircraft well away from large crowds. With the help of a friend named Torrence Huffman, they established their flying base at the Huffman Prairie, some 10 miles (16km) from Dayton. Here, in the second half of 1904, the *Flyer II* took to the air about 75 times, the best flight covering just under 3 miles (4.8km) in 5 minutes 4 seconds. Just as importantly, on 20 September Wilbur Wright succeeded in flying a circle, an achievement that had eluded the brothers up to that time because their aircraft had not climbed high enough to be banked safely.

A refinement in the Wrights' technique had been introduced earlier in September, when they started using an accelerator device for the take-off trolley. This device consisted of a heavy weight winched to the top of a derrick. Here it was attached to the tail of a rope that was led via pulleys to the front of the launching rail and then back to the trolley. The weight was released to drop to the ground so that the rope drew the trolley swiftly forward along the rail. This device enabled the Wrights to fly on days when there was little wind, since the *Flyer* would have been unable to reach flying speed relative to the wind along the rail.

The brothers were seen in the air by some hundreds of people, and on two occasions reporters came to the field to investigate the reports of flight. By a quirk of nature, the engine failed to start on both of these visits, and the pressmen went away sceptical.

The next year, 1905, witnessed the emergence of the definitive, fully airworthy Wright aeroplane, the *Flyer III*. Again the same basic design was retained,

this time with a span of 40ft 6in (12.35m), but to improve the effectiveness of the elevators and the rudders they were moved farther from the wings. Some 40 flights were made between June and October, and in this period the brothers perfected their flying technique. The one problem still plaguing them was a tendency for the aeroplane to stall in turns. This was seen to be the result of the wing on the inner side of the turn slowing and thereby losing lift. The answer was simple: merely push the nose down slightly in turns and thus keep speed up. At the same time the permanent link between the warp cradle and the rudder controls was abandoned, enabling the pilot to use the two controls separately should he so desire, or to co-ordinate them in different ratios and thus produce a greater variety of banked turns. With the engine running reliably and powerfully, the *Flyer III* can certainly be called the first truly practical aeroplane in history.

The considerable performance improvement of the *Flyer III* over the *Flyer II* can be gauged easily from the impressive number of flights of more than 15 minutes' duration made during the summer: there were six such flights and these included two of more than 30 minutes. The year's best flight was made on 5 October, when the *Flyer III* was airborne for 38 minutes 3 seconds, in which time it covered more than 24 miles (38.6km). The machine was therefore undeniably capable of sustained flight. Added to this, the fact that no major damage was done in 40 take-offs and landings bears eloquent witness to the *Flyer III*'s sturdiness. Perhaps the most important factor, however, was that the two pilots were able to manoeuvre the

aeroplane in a fully practical manner.

The confidence of the Wright brothers that they had capped six years of development work with a viable aircraft is reflected in the fact that they offered it to both the American and British governments. Patents for the most important elements of the *Flyer* were pending, and the brothers now felt that they could begin to profit from their invention. In January 1905 the brothers had offered their machine to the US Department of War, while they were still building the *Flyer III*: the Department turned the offer down without even considering it. The brothers then approached the British War Office. So slowly did the administrative mills of that body grind that in October, after the performance of the *Flyer III* had been fully tested, the American brothers abandoned the attempt for another approach to the US Department of War. Although the Wrights made it clear that they were offering a machine with guaranteed aerial performance, the Department of War insisted on treating the offer as a request for assistance, and again turned down the offer.

The lead the USA had attained in the field of aviation can be judged by the fact that the first European aeroplane to fly, although in reality this effort was no more than a hop, did not take to the air for nearly another 12 months. This lead was now to be lost as a result of the short-sightedness of the government. So discouraged were the Wrights, and so fearful that their ideas might be stolen before their patents came through in 1906, that they ceased flying and development work on their aircraft for the next 30 months. The *Flyer III* was locked away in a shed and no one was allowed to

examine it. The Wrights even refused to allow drawings of it to be made, although a fairly accurate sketch appeared in the Paris paper, *L'Auto*, on Christmas Eve 1905 after being stolen in Dayton. Nevertheless, the aeroplane remained on sale: the brothers guaranteed the performance, but would allow no one to see the machine or plans until they had bought them. So until 1908 the brothers made no future progress, although in the interval they built a few improved engines and a small number of *Flyer III* machines in the definitive form known as the Model A, against the day that either the government or commercial interests decided to consider the aeroplane seriously.

In six years these two American brothers had undertaken the research, designed and built the airframes, engines and propellers of a series of gliders and powered aircraft, culminating in the first practical aeroplane, and taught themselves to fly their machines with great proficiency. And then they stopped.

OPPOSITE
Orville Wright is seen aloft in the Wright Model A biplane over Fort Myer outside Washington, DC, during 1908. Such flights helped to convince the American public and military that flight was indeed a reality.

Chapter Two

Primitive Flying Machines

In Europe only slow progress was made towards the goal of powered flight, which is surprising since the decade up to the turn of the century had been particularly fruitful, and air-mindedness was widespread. The year 1900 found only one European, the French officer Capitaine Ferdinand Ferber, actively pursuing the search for flight. In January 1902 Ferber forsook the Lilienthal type of glider when he received information from Chanute about the Wrights' gliders. He immediately began construction of a Wright-type glider, but with only limited information on which to work his effort was a failure. One of the principal reasons for this failure was the fact that the wing surfaces were not rigid and therefore produced virtually no lift. After Chanute had delivered a lecture to the Aéro-Club de France in April 1903, in the process displaying drawings and photographs of the Wrights' No. 3 Glider, Ferber returned to work with renewed enthusiasm. He was again unsuccessful, but did initiate a design feature of considerable importance: not satisfied with the Wright's inherent instability, Ferber designed his 1904 glider with dihedralled wings and, more significantly, a fixed horizontal tailplane to improve longitudinal stability. This was a major step in the right direction but, in

common with most other Europeans, Ferber ignored the question of control in roll and instead relied on dihedralled wings for lateral stability. This was to be a stumbling block of major proportions until 1908, when Wilbur Wright demonstrated his Model A in France, and the true nature of the Wright glider's skill in full

lateral control was revealed.

The man who next took the lead in European progress was the French lawyer Ernest Archdeacon, who was encouraged by the Chanute lecture to persevere both by forming an aviation committee within the Aéro-Club de France and by ordering a copy of the Wright glider. This copy was

Seen in the control car of one of his fascinating little dirigibles, with the skeleton of a hangar in the background, the expatriate Brazilian flyer Alberto Santos-Dumont was to a great extent responsible for the creation and nurture of a practical air-mindedness in France in the last decade of the 19th century and the first decade of the 20th century.

ready in 1904, and it was flown by Ferber and Gabriel Voisin. Another Frenchman inspired by the Wrights was Robert Esnault-Peltérie, who decided that he could improve upon the Wrights' glider since he thought that wing warping was structurally dangerous. In common with other French experimenters, Esnault-Pelérie did not fully understand the nature of lateral control as developed by the Wrights, but he nonetheless has the distinction of being the first man to have used ailerons. As with all the other French copies of the Wright glider, that of Esnault-Pelérie was a relative failure. Yet, oddly enough, French experimenters were content to move on to powered flight without attempting even to understand, let alone correct, the shortcomings of their gliders.

In 1905 the French finally abandoned the Wright type of glider, thereby setting themselves back in the short term, after a lecture by Esnault-Peltérie in which he stated that he had built an exact copy of the No. 3 Glider and that it would not fly in the fashion claimed by the brothers, and had then improved the design by installing ailerons. The only conclusion possible, according to Esnault-Peltérie, was that the Wrights were at the least exaggerating their successes. Some progress was made in 1905, however. Early in the year Archdeacon had another Wright-type glider built. But following the lead of Ferber, fixed vertical and horizontal tail surfaces were added. The glider was not piloted, but in two car-towed tests it seemed to behave well until there was a structural failure in the tail unit. With considerable help from Voisin, Archdeacon now built a new glider that was to introduce the Hargrave box-kite to European aviation. This was basically a Wright-type glider, fitted with a forward elevator and a two-cell box-kite mounted on booms behind the wings to provide longitudinal and directional stability. The main biplane wings were divided into three cells by side-curtains round each set of interplane struts. With Voisin at the controls the whole machine was mounted on floats and towed into the air over the River Seine by a motorboat, on the second flight recording a distance of almost 1,000ft (300m).

In 1905 Ferber made his mark on history with the first free flight by a powered aeroplane in Europe, and the first tractor biplane in the world. The machine in question was the Ferber VII-B, basically similar to his earlier adaptation of the Wright glider with a horizontal tail, and a 12-hp (8.9-kW)

engine added between the wing leading edge and the forward elevator. Released from an overhead wire once flying speed had been reached, the Ferber VII-B could achieve only what might be described as a powered glide when it was tested on 25 May. The machine had no adequate lateral control, and Ferber still favoured a floating horizontal tail, unsupported by wire bracing so that it might move up or down in flight. Although his machine was unsuccessful, Ferber had made an extremely significant contribution to aviation with his invention of the tractor biplane layout.

The French thought that their major task for 1906 would have to be the overtaking of the Wrights so that France would secure the honour of being the country to have made the first powered heavier-than-air flight. With the French publication during January 1906 of major portions of the Wrights' wing warping and rudder control patent, complete with drawings, the French were for the first time in possession of the basic element of the Wrights' success, but greeted this potential revelation with complete indifference: indeed, in the August number of *L'Aérophile* magazine one of the more dynamic of French pioneers, Archdeacon, demanded a radical shake-up

It was in the extraordinarily inelegant No. 14-bis, in which he stood to operate the controls, that Alberto Santos-Dumont achieved the first flight (in reality little more than a hop) in Europe. The date was 12 November 1906, and at the time the French credited this as the first flight anywhere in the world.

of the French aeronautical world, pointing out that a suitably powerful engine, with a good power/weight ratio, was now available in the form of the Levavasseur Antoinette, and all that was needed to enable the French to redress the slight lead held by the Wrights was a solution to the problem of balance and control. In common with all his countrymen, Archdeacon had entirely overlooked the significance of the feature on the Wrights' patent in the January edition of *L'Aérophile*. As a spur to French efforts, Archdeacon again reminded his readers of the offer he had made in 1904 of a Prix Deutsch-Archdeacon for the first man to fly a circular course of 1 km (0.6 mile). Perhaps to discourage his readers from setting their sights on smaller targets, Archdeacon made no mention of the prizes that he had offered at much the same time for flights of only 25 and 100m (27.5 and 110yards). Nevertheless, the year 1906 was to see the winning of these last two prizes, though the third prize was to remain unclaimed until the beginning of 1908.

The engine Archdeacon had discussed in his article was designed by one of the unsung heroes of aviation, Léon Levavasseur. This man, who named his famous Antoinette engine after the daughter of Jules Gastambide, the head of his firm, originally created the unit in 1903 for racing motorboats. Levavasseur's two basic engines, of 25 and 50hp (18.6 and 37.3kW), powered most of the important European aircraft up to 1909. By the standards of the day the engines were reliable, and their racing heritage had given them a good power/weight ratio in the region of 4.2lb/hp (2.55kg/kW). Only with the

advent of the Gnome rotary, designed by Laurent Séguin in 1907 and introduced from late 1908 onwards, would the Antoinette 50-hp (37.3-kW) engine be superseded as the prime mover of European aircraft.

The first man in Europe who can really be said to have flown was neither a European nor a pioneer previously interested in heavier-than-air flight. Alberto Santos-Dumont was a diminutive Brazilian whose family had become affluent in the coffee trade and was thus able to settle in France and pursue his love of airships before the turn of the century. Persevering despite innumerable setbacks and accidents, Santos-Dumont at last evolved a workable type of miniature dirigible before, in 1905, developing an interest in heavier-than-air flying machines. His first machine, which was to be the first European aeroplane to fly, was a machine that was bizarre even by the standards of the times, and totally without further influence on the development of flight. Perhaps inspired by Langley, Santos-Dumont described his machine as an *aérodrome* rather than as an *avion*, the word coined by Ader and now coming into general use in France. The Santos-Dumont 14-bis, as it came to

achieved the first recognized flight in Europe by flying 722ft (220m) in 21.2 seconds at an altitude of some 20ft (6m). Although only about a third of what the Wrights had managed on their first days flying in December 1903, this was enough to win Santos-Dumont wild acclaim in Paris, and warm congratulations poured in from all over the world. Various sectors of the community now began to take an interest in aviation. Foremost among them was the champagne industry based in Reims, spearheaded by the firm of Ruinart. On 4 December 1906 this company offered a prize of 12,500 francs for the first man to fly across the English Channel. This was a very farsighted offer, and typical of the encouragement the champagne industry was to offer aviation over the next few years.

Despite the French feeling that the air had now been conquered, in the following year only Henry Farman achieved anything like proficiency in the air. Although of English birth, Farman had lived all his life in France and spoke virtually no English. Farman was one of the several buyers of the pusher biplanes built by the Voisin brothers. The Voisins habitually designated their machines only by the name of the customer, but as the brothers themselves played such an important part in the designs, their types should also include their own name in any realistic nomenclature. The basic Voisin aircraft was essentially a Chanute type of biplane wing with a Wright forward elevator and a Hargrave box-kite tail. This basic design, less the Wright element, was tested and refined as a hang-glider in May 1907.

Little is known of the very first powered aeroplane built by the Voisins.

be known by reason of the fact that it was tested under Santos-Dumont's No. 14 airship, was designed and built near Paris in 1906. It was of canard configuration, that is with the normal positions of wings and tail assembly reversed, and power was provided by a 25-hp (18.6-kW) Antoinette engine mounted at the rear of the fuselage and driving a pusher propeller. First tests were undertaken in June 1906, the aeroplane being suspended from a wire on a pulley and towed by a donkey!

It is hardly surprising that no worthwhile results were achieved. July witnessed the first air tests under the No. 14 airship, and the first attempt at free flight was made on 13 September. After a hop of only 23ft (7m) the 14-bis came down heavily and suffered major damage.

While the machine was being repaired, Santos-Dumont also changed the engine for a more powerful 50-hp (37.3-kW) Antoinette and then attempted his second flight on 23 October. This time he managed to achieve a hop of 198ft (60m), thereby winning the Archdeacon prize for the first flight of 25m. Realizing that some form of lateral control was necessary, Santos-Dumont next modified the 14-bis to incorporate a pair of large ailerons, operated by a harness worn round the pilot's body, mounted between the wings in the outermost bracing bay of each pair of wings, each of which had three side-curtains. All was ready for Santos-Dumont's greatest triumph, on 12 November 1906. After five short hops, the best of which covered 270ft (82m) in 7.2 seconds, Santos-Dumont finally

This resulted from a commission from Henry Kapferer, basically a lighter-than-air enthusiast. Power was provided by a 25-hp (18.6-kW) Buchet engine, with which the aeroplane could not possibly have flown. In terms of basic layout the Voisin-Delagrange I seems to have been similar to what is known of the Voisin-Kapferer. The aeroplane had a shoe-shaped nacelle, or body, mounted on the lower wing, with the 50-hp (37.3-kW) Antoinette driving a pusher propeller directly at its rear. The pilot and controls were in the centre, and the biplane forward elevator was located at the front. The biplane wings had no side-curtains, and a two-cell tailplane, mounted on four booms running back from the wings, carried two rudders hinged to the rear of

its outer side-curtains. In this form the Voisin-Delagrange I took off six times in March and April 1906, but the best hop was only 198ft (60m). The machine was then modified at Archdeacon's suggestion, and also fitted with floats. Thus altered, the type failed to take off at all when tested on the Lac d'Enghien in spring, and was again taken in hand for modifications. The float alighting gear was replaced by wheeled landing gear, and the two rudders replaced by a single central rudder. With Delagrange replacing Charles Voisin as the pilot, the aeroplane took off twice early in November, the second of these flights proving to be the best made by a European to date, covering 1,640ft (500m). Unhappily, Delagrange crashed on landing and the aeroplane was destroyed. The Voisins' third powered aeroplane set the pattern which the two brothers were to copy with increasing success up to 1910. The machine in question was built to the order of Henry Farman, and is now known as the Voisin-Farman I. Ordered in the middle of 1907, it was delivered in October. In its first form it closely resembled the Voisin-Delagrange I, with the exception of a slightly greater wing span and a tailplane with a central rudder but with no central curtain. The machine was considerably heavier than its Delagrange counterpart, and this was probably the result of structural strengthening.

Although generally happy with the first tests, Farman instructed the Voisins to re-rig the aircraft with dihedral to increase its lateral stability, and to replace the biplane elevators with a monoplane unit. With these alterations the Voisin-Farman I flew 2,530ft (771m) in 52.6 seconds on 26 October. Though this was

a European record, it was just one month short of four years after the Wrights' first flights, and did not even equal the time of their fourth flight. Farman, not yet satisfied with his machine, ordered that the original large tailplane be replaced by a unit of reduced span. As the Voisin-Farman I (Modified), the aeroplane now flew well and at last the Europeans could be said to have something approaching a practical aeroplane. The basic soundness of the Voisins' combination of Wright, Chanute and Hargrave elements, as modified by Farman, was soon proved by Farman's flight of 3,400ft (1030m) in a circle, in a time of 1 minute 14 seconds. This won an Archdeacon prize for a flight of more than 150m, neither Santos-Dumont's nor Delagrange's flights having been scrutinized by the relevant officials.

For the next few years Farman was in the vanguard of biplane development, but even he had not as yet appreciated fully the need for lateral control rather than lateral stability. The circular flight he had made on 9 November clearly demonstrated this need: to turn his aeroplane Farman had to skid it round, and at the slow speeds of only about 34mph (55km/h), the wing on the inside of the turn must have been very close to stalling. His low altitude would have given Farman no chance of recovering had this happened, even if he had known what to do. Because of his slow speed and extremely low altitude, however, Farman might well have been able to simply walk away from a crash as had some others.

After several years of experimentation with various types, Louis Blériot finally came in 1907 to adopt the tractor monoplane, the type that was to make

monoplane and reached its definitive, if rudimentary, form. There were no control surfaces forward of the mainplanes, but there were both fixed and movable directional and longitudinal tail surfaces. In common with most other European machines of its era there was no understanding of the need for lateral control, and Alfred de Pischoff's biplane featured neither ailerons nor wing warping. Although the aeroplane failed to fly, it is still of considerable importance for, apart from introducing the tractor biplane layout, the de Pischoff I incorporated two important innovations. The more important of these was the propeller, designed and made by Lucien Chauvière, who also built the aeroplane: this propeller was a built-up wooden structure of considerable efficiency, and presaged the dominance of this propeller type for years to come. It was still not as advanced as the Wrights' propeller, but this deficiency would be rectified in the next two years. The de Pischoff I also introduced the 25-hp (18.6-kW) arrowhead Anzani engine, in which the V of the outer two cylinders was bisected by an upright third cylinder. Blériot's

him famous. As had been his practice with other layouts, Blériot progressed cautiously and logically, and it was not until after he had discarded two designs that he arrived at the one now considered the definitive form, with an enclosed fuselage, tractor engine, forward-mounted wings, and empennage at the rear of the

fuselage. The elevators were in fact elevons, for Blériot had not realized that to make them efficient, ailerons must be placed as far as possible from the fuselage centreline. Power was provided by a sterling 50-hp (37.3-kW) Antoinette which enabled the Blériot VII to take off several times at the close of 1907, two of

the flights covering more than 1,640ft (500m). And although the Blériot VII was not a successful type in itself, with it Blériot had arrived at the starting point of the line of monoplanes he was to make world famous.

With the de Pischoff I, built in 1907, the tractor biplane emulated the tractor

monoplanes were to take on a new lease of life with this efficient powerplant.

Two Austrians entered the field of aviation in 1907, with important consequences for the future. Igo Etrich and Franz Wels were fascinated by bird flight, and designed an aeroplane based on a bird's wing planform. It was intended that the monoplane should be flown with an Antoinette engine, but the type was first tested with some success as a glider. Etrich, the more important of the partners, further developed this planform, and it was to become celebrated in the series of bird-like monoplanes developed in the years just before the outbreak of World War I which were extensively copied all over Europe, and were emulated especially in Germany.

It was not until 1908 that the public was first to witness aviators who could not only make small hops, but could also launch themselves into the air and stay there for considerable periods, controlling their aircraft fully, making them climb, dive, circle, bank and otherwise perform as an expert rider might make a horse conform to his will. The general impact of this was very great; but it was greater still on the aviators and would-be aviators of Europe and America. For the first time they had incontrovertible proof that full flight was possible, and that the key to flight was not lift combined with inherent stability, but controllability combined with lift. As in the previous year, it was the biplane, mostly of the pusher variety, that led the way, although the monoplane now began to show its true worth, particularly the Blériot and Antoinette types.

Of the biplane enthusiasts, it was Delagrange and Farman who were best able to capitalize on their moderate previous successes. On 13 January 1908, Farman completed a round flight of more than 1km (0.6mile). Flying his Voisin-Farman I (Modified), he repeated the flight he had made at the end of 1907, witnessed this time by the requisite officials, and so collected the Grand Prix d'Aviation Deutsch-Archdeacon of 50,000 francs. It is interesting to note that Farman's round trip of 1km was in fact nearer 1.5km (0.9mile) for the simple reason that without lateral control he could not merely bank round the marker at the far end of his course, but rather

marginal at first, but Delagrange began to worry about lateral stability after a crash on 3 May. Consequently the aeroplane was modified as the Voisin-Delagrange III, with curtains on the two innermost sets of interplane struts. Although it made the machine look slightly strange, the curtains seem to have had the desired effect, and Delagrange managed several useful flights in Italy. The best of these flights, on 23 June, took Delagrange 8.87 miles (14.27km) in 18 minutes 30 seconds. Like Farman, Delagrange made two passenger flights, and it is noticeable that the two pilots were closely paralleling each other in their achievements.

Other European adherents to the biplane were not faring as well, however. In France, Ferber had joined the Antoinette concern, and his last machine was designated the Ferber IX and also Antoinette III. This was an extremely ungainly tractor biplane, from above resembling nothing so much as a fish skeleton since the wing ribs were uncovered on top. A forward elevator was provided, and at this stage Ferber abandoned his idea of a floating tail in favour of a fixed one. Two completely useless rudders were hinged to the outermost rear interplane struts, but they were soon changed for a more conventional one on the empennage. The Ferber IX actually rose from the ground on eight occasions, and on its last flight the machine covered 1,640ft (500m) before crashing. Ferber then abandoned the type.

The establishment of the Aerial Experiment Association (AEA) in the USA during September 1907 by Dr A. Graham Bell and his wife, with the newcomer Glenn Curtiss as its prime

had to skid round it in a wide curve. Farman made several comparable flights in the next two days before taking apart his machine for the reconstruction and modification he now decided was necessary. The modified aeroplane, now designated the Voisin-Farman I-bis, was ready for flight in March. Little had been done in the way of modifying the basic airframe, but a new engine, a 50-hp (37.3-kW) Renault, had been installed and the aeroplane was completely recovered with rubberized linen to replace the silk of the Voisin-Farman I (Modified). The Renault engine was used

only once: Farman found it unsatisfactory and reverted to the original Antoinette. With the old engine once again installed, the Voisin-Farman I-bis began to show its paces, unspectacular as they were soon to appear in comparison with those of Wilbur Wright's machine. On 21 March Farman flew just over 1.2 miles (2km) in 3 minutes 31 seconds. In May, while in Ghent in Belgium, Farman took Archdeacon for two flights which constituted the first passenger flights in Europe. Farman was then invited to the USA, but his trip proved almost totally abortive for a variety of reasons, and he

wasted the months of July and August. Before his departure on this venture, however, Farman succeeded in making the longest flight to date in Europe when on 6 July he stayed in the air for 20 minutes 20 seconds.

Delagrange, meanwhile, was close on Farman's heels. With his old machine virtually written off in November 1907, Delagrange ordered another machine from the Voisins. This incorporated what could be salvaged from the Voisin-Delagrange I, and emerged as the Voisin-Delagrange II. Differences between this and the Voisin-Farman I (Modified) were mover, was an event of considerable importance. During 1908, the AEA built and tested three similar biplanes, the *Red Wing*, the *White Wing* and the *June Bug*. The *Red Wing*, designed by Lieutenant T.E. Selfridge, was powered by the excellent Curtiss engine. Essentially a Wright-type machine adapted with horizontal tail surfaces and fitted with skid landing gear as it was tested from the frozen surface of Lake Keuka, the *Red Wing* had an unusual wing layout, the lower wing having pronounced, curved dihedral, and the upper wing similarly pronounced, curved anhedral, so that the two wingtips came close to each other. The intention was presumably to get the benefit of both dihedral and a form of side-curtain. Only two flights were made, with F.W. Baldwin as pilot, the first on 12 March being the better, covering 319ft (97m). The second effort resulted in a crash and the *Red Wing* was abandoned in favour of the *White Wing* design by Baldwin. The *White Wing* was similar to its predecessor, but had conventional landing gear and ailerons. Five flights were made in May, the best covering 1,017ft (310m). Like the *Red Wing*, the *White Wing* was given up after a crash landing and succeeded by the *June Bug*, a design by Curtiss. Like the two previous aircraft, this was powered by the Curtiss engine, and retained the distinctive curved wings. This time four ailerons were fitted, and the tail surfaces were improved by being made into a biplane structure. Flown by Curtiss himself and by J.A. McCurdy who like Baldwin was a Canadian, the *June Bug* proved itself far superior to the two earlier aircraft. Some 30 flights were made, the most notable being one of 2 miles (3.2km) on 29 August. With the *June Bug* Curtiss won the prize offered by the *Scientific*

American magazine for the first flight of over 0.6 mile (1km), with an effort of 5,090ft (1551m) in 1 minute 42.5 seconds. Curtiss, who had recently fallen foul of the Wright brothers because of his infringement of their 1906 warping patent, was also able to bank the *June Bug* round in a circle.

After Blériot's introduction of the classic monoplane layout in 1907, further progress was made in 1908 towards turning this type into a viable flying

machine, although complete success was to evade the two major monoplane designers until 1909. These two designers were Blériot and Levavasseur, the latter being both chief engineer and founder of the Antoinette firm.

Blériot quickly moved towards the finalized form of monoplane with his No. VIII, completed in June 1908. In its first form the No. VIII spanned 36ft 1in (11m) but this was soon cut down to 27ft 10in (8.5m). Power was provided by a 50-hp

(37.3-kW) Antoinette, and although the fuselage was at first covered, the designer soon altered this and the No. VIII took on the open-fuselage form so distinctive in Blériot monoplanes. The tail controls were conventional, except that it was the outer, rather than the rear portions of the horizontal tail surface that moved to give longitudinal control. With Blériot at last on the right lines, swift progress could be expected, and Blériot turned in a flight of 2,997ft (900m) on 29 June, the last day

OPPOSITE

OPPOSITE
Most of the pioneers of flight has to exploit every possible source of revenue to sustain their efforts. One of the most successful and popular enterprises was what would now be termed air experience flights. This shows the German pilot Siegfried Hoffmann with four passengers before a flight in 1914.

BELOW
Once the possibility of successful flight had been fully confirmed, the emphasis switched to the creation of aircraft that could fly ever faster, higher and farther. This placed greater emphasis on powerful engines, stronger structures and aerodynamically cleaner airframes. The last word in high-speed aircraft before World War I was the Deperdussin Monocoque racer, which established a world air speed record of 126.7mph (203.8km/h) in September 1913.

on which the No. VIII flew in its original form. The modifications envisaged by the designer involved the ailerons. On the original model these had been triangular, but Blériot now replaced them with far more efficient rectangular units mounted as the trailing portion of each outer wing panel. The ailerons could only move downwards, so only one could be used at any one time. It was clear that Blériot had made the right decision when flight trials with what was now designated the No. VIII-bis were resumed in July, and on 6 July the No. VIII-bis remained airborne for 8 minutes 24 seconds. Still not satisfied, Blériot continued to experiment with the controls. In September he modified the No. VIII-bis into the No. VIII-ter by replacing the rectangular flap-type ailerons with differential elevons

formed on the outer ends of the wings, and at the same time added a fixed horizontal tail surface. Yet again, Blériot's modifications proved efficient, the No. VIII-ter making a 2.78-mile (4.5-km) flight on 2 October. On 31 October, Blériot made a round trip of about 17.4 miles (28km), with two landings, in 22 minutes. Still greater advances were to be expected from Blériot in 1909.

It was in 1908, too, that

Levavasseur's monoplane first appeared. Although the first Antoinette aircraft were rather ungainly machines, Levavasseur was then to develop his basic idea into a series of extremely elegant aircraft, far excelling those of Blériot in purely aesthetic qualities. Levavasseur's active interest in flight had begun in 1903, when he built the first petrol-engined aeroplane to be freely tested in France. The machine was a failure, but this fact did not deter

Levavasseur, who re-entered the field with the Gastambide-Mengin I ordered by his employer and another member of the firm in 1907, and delivered in February 1908. The aeroplane, although unsuccessful, was interesting in one very important respect: the aerofoil section of the wings. Up to this date most early aerofoils had consisted of parallel-sided cambered surfaces. Levavasseur, however, followed the example of the British pioneer

Horatio Phillips and adopted a section with considerably less camber on the under-surface. This produced as much lift as the parallel-sided aerofoils, but far less drag. The wing of the Gastambide-Mengin I was pleasantly tapered, but the fuselage was massive and perched on an ungainly four-wheeled landing gear arrangement. The 50-hp (37.3-kW) engine was mounted in the nose and drove an inefficient paddle-bladed propeller. Intended basically as a test vehicle, the aeroplane had no control surfaces at all. Only four tests were made, all piloted by an Antoinette mechanic called Boyer, the best covering some 492ft (150m). After a crash-landing the aeroplane was reconstructed, appearing as the Gastambide-Mengin II, or more properly the Antoinette II, in July. Large triangular ailerons were added to the rear of the outer wing panels, and an elevator and twin rudders were installed. Now piloted by another member of the Société Antoinette, Welferinger, the Antoinette II proved moderately successful and its best

flight during large-scale trials in July and August lasted 1 minute 36 seconds. Welferinger also took Gastambide for a flight, and completed a circle in the air, both events being firsts for monoplanes. Levavasseur had no part, as far as is known, in the Antoinette III, otherwise designated the Ferber IX. His next aeroplane, the Antoinette IV, was the world's first truly successful monoplane. This graceful machine was completed in October 1908, and in the course of a career that was lengthy by contemporary standards, it underwent a series of modifications, especially to the landing gear. As most attention at the time was concentrated on this machine's successor, the Antoinette V, it is impossible to trace all the modifications for lack of evidence. Nevertheless, the Antoinette IV ushered in the era of graceful Levavasseur monoplanes, the majority of them featuring a boat-shaped fuselage of triangular section, probably inspired by Levavasseur's earlier association with racing motor-boats.

During 1908 the whole tenor of European aviation was altered by one factor: the flying of Wilbur Wright in France. At the beginning of the year the Wrights' relationship with the aeronautical world took on a healthier aspect when the brothers contracted to provide an aeroplane and pilot training for the US Army's Signal Corps, and to have their aircraft built under licence in France. It was decided that while Orville conducted the Signal Corps evaluation and acceptance trials, Wilbur should go to France to demonstrate the aeroplane already sent over in July 1907. Both the Signal Corps and French aircraft were of the batch built after the brothers had given up flying in 1905, and were of the modified *Flyer III* design called the Flyer Model A. Although the Wrights themselves did not use this appellation, they did call their next basic type the Flyer Model B. Orville and Wilbur had brushed up their flying techniques on the *Flyer III*, modified to Model A standard by the provision of two upright seats and other refinements, during May 1908. Immediately afterward, Wilbur took ship for France to collect the crated Model A from the docks at Le Havre. He then moved on to Le Mans, where he set about assembling the Model A in a factory. Because of delays the reassembly took longer than expected, but all was ready early in August.

Naturally enough, the French aviation world was following Wilbur's progress with interest. Unruffled and methodical as ever, Wilbur was so confident in the machine and his work that he made no private test flights before announcing that he would take to the air on 8 August. The crowd at Hunaudières racecourse near Le Mans on that day included many

of the ablest minds in French aviation, who watched with fascination as the launching rail was laid into the wind, the aeroplane installed on the trolley, the weight hauled to the top of the derrick, and the launching rope connected. Wilbur gave the signal and the Model A accelerated smoothly down the rail and rose gracefully into the air. Wilbur climbed, circled round twice, his superb banking showing off the degree of control possible with the use of warping and rudder control, and then landed after a flight of only 1 minute 45 seconds. The crowd was astounded, even those who had expressed a belief in the brothers' claims being overwhelmed by the magnitude of the event. It was not that Wilbur's flight had excelled in hard facts anything that the Europeans had done, but rather that it had been of a quality hitherto the subject of dreams rather than actuality.

Wilbur continued to astonish for the next six days at Hunaudières, and then moved to the military training ground at the Camp d'Auvours, east of Le Mans. He flew from here for the rest of the year, putting in some 26 hours in the air between 8 August and the end of 1908. On 60 of his flights Wilbur took up passengers, and among other notable flights he made six lasting between one and two hours, and on the last day of the year stayed aloft for a remarkable 2 hours 20 minutes 23 seconds. He also secured the world altitude record at 361ft (110m). By the end of the year the Wrights' achievements in previous years had been recognized, and Wilbur Wright was a celebrity all over Europe. Indeed, other celebrities, not merely fellow aviation enthusiasts, flocked to the Camp d'Auvours to see the wonder of the year.

OPPOSITE
The Avro Type 504 was developed before World War I and remained in service into the 1930s as a trainer with viceless handling characteristics and beautifully harmonized controls. In the first stages of World War I the type was used for offensive flights, this being the aeroplane in which Wing Commander E.F. Briggs of the Royal Naval Air Service bombed the Zeppelin sheds at Friedrichshafen in southern Germany during November 1914.

LEFT
The final development of the Avro Type 504 was in a number of variants optimized for the training role, as epitomized by this Type 504K.

While Wilbur had his triumphs in Europe, Orville at first enjoyed similar acclaim in the USA. The Model A was assembled at Fort Myer outside Washington, DC, and Orville began acceptance trials under Signal Corps supervision on 3 September, immediately impressing all who saw him in the air with his complete mastery of flight. Progress was smooth and rapid: Orville made four flights of more than one hour, created two altitude records and took up passengers on three occasions. But on 17 September all this came to an end. Late in the afternoon, Orville had taken Lieutenant T.E. Selfridge, one of the leading lights of the AEA, on an official flight. As they circled the field, one of the blades of the starboard propeller cracked along its length, then hit and cut one of the wires bracing the rudders. As Orville throttled back and tried to land the rudder structure collapsed, causing the aeroplane to dive into the ground. Selfridge was killed instantly, and Orville was badly injured. He was back on his feet fairly soon, however, and went to France to join Wilbur. Selfridge was the first person to be killed in a powered aeroplane, and only the fourth aviator to be killed since serious work into heavier-than-air flight had begun during the last century.

On Henry Farman's return to France from the USA, where the news of Wilbur Wright's French triumphs had overtaken him, Farman set about modifying his Voisin-Farman I-bis into the Farman I-bis (Modified) by fitting four side-curtains to make individual cells of each outer wing bay. With this machine Farman now managed to make some good flights, including three lasting over 30 minutes. Being a natural airman, Farman had for some time had an inkling of what was wrong with his aircraft, and consideration of Wilbur Wright's flying made him realize suddenly that lateral control was the element missing from his Farman I-bis (Modified). Early in October, therefore, Farman installed four large ailerons, one inset into each of the outer wing panels. Although these could only move downwards, Farman had evolved the first truly efficient ailerons ever fitted. Thus improved, the aeroplane performed creditably, and on 30 October Farman made the world's first true cross-country flight, of 16.8 miles (27km) in 20 minutes.

Farman's successes, and the Wrights' flights in France, mark the end of an era in aviation history. The experimenters, or most of them, were no longer working with a mixture of hope and desperation: they had a basis of understanding and practicality from which to develop. The sudden leap in the numbers of successes during 1909 and the increase in public enthusiasm for aviation and aviation meetings were entirely due to the foundations laid in these earlier years.

Chapter Three
Annus Mirabilis –
The Year of the Reims Meeting

Two factors were eventually to assist European pioneers in overhauling the Wrights and taking over the lead in world aviation. Firstly, Wilbur's demonstration flying had revealed that full three-axis flight control was essential and, secondly, the belief of the European pioneers in their own capabilities had been greatly put out by the universal acclaim that Orville and Wilbur Wright had received.

The Wright brothers had decided right from the beginning that inherent instability was what was needed to produce the true flying machine, while the Europeans had tended to the opposite view that inherent stability was essential. The Wrights wished to be able to exercise total control over their creation, while the Europeans wished to be able to drive theirs. The Wrights were correct to insist on control, and the Europeans were correct in wishing to ensure a measure of inherent stability, but whereas the American brothers would not budge from their preconception, from 1908 onward the Europeans swiftly realized that they would have a viable and safe machine if they could combine their ideas about stability with those of the Wrights on controllability. Virtually the only Europeans to fail to understand this lesson were Gabriel and Charles Voisin,

whose designs went into a temporary limbo from this point onwards, even though they continued to prosper with sales of their proven but now outmoded designs.

The Wright brothers continued to play an important part in the realization of practical aviation over the next two years, but their basic *Flyer* design was fast approaching the end of its useful development life, and the brothers had little but drastic revisions of the original type with which to replace it. Too late

they realized that they were beginning to fall from the cutting edge of aviation development, and by the end of 1909 Europe was firmly established as the centre of the aeronautical world. Aircraft of the *Flyer* type demanded piloting of great skill: the machine could not be left to its own devices in the air for even a few seconds, so the strain on the pilot during any but the shortest flights was considerable. Most of the emerging generation of pilots, attracted by the publicity that had attended the first

European successes and Wilbur Wright's French tour, wanted to get into the air as quickly as possible. For them the Wright type of aeroplane was wholly unsuitable, and so they bought Voisin types, graduating on to less stable but fully controllable European machines once they had mastered the basic techniques.

The most important part of the Europeans' development of controlled

LEFT
There can be little doubt that the early days of flight attracted men and women of character, this being Lieutenant Colonel Bouttieaux, the French director of air equipment in 1911, seated behind the pilot.

OPPOSITE
Until a time quite late in the development of successful flight, extravagant claims were made for the extraordinary machine created by Sir Hiram Maxim in 1894. This steam-powered behemoth had a biplane wing cellule and developed sufficient lift for the machine to break free through the planks that were designed to prevent it from rising above the tracks on which it ran, but never flew as such as it was designed only for the investigation of lift and therefore had no control surfaces.

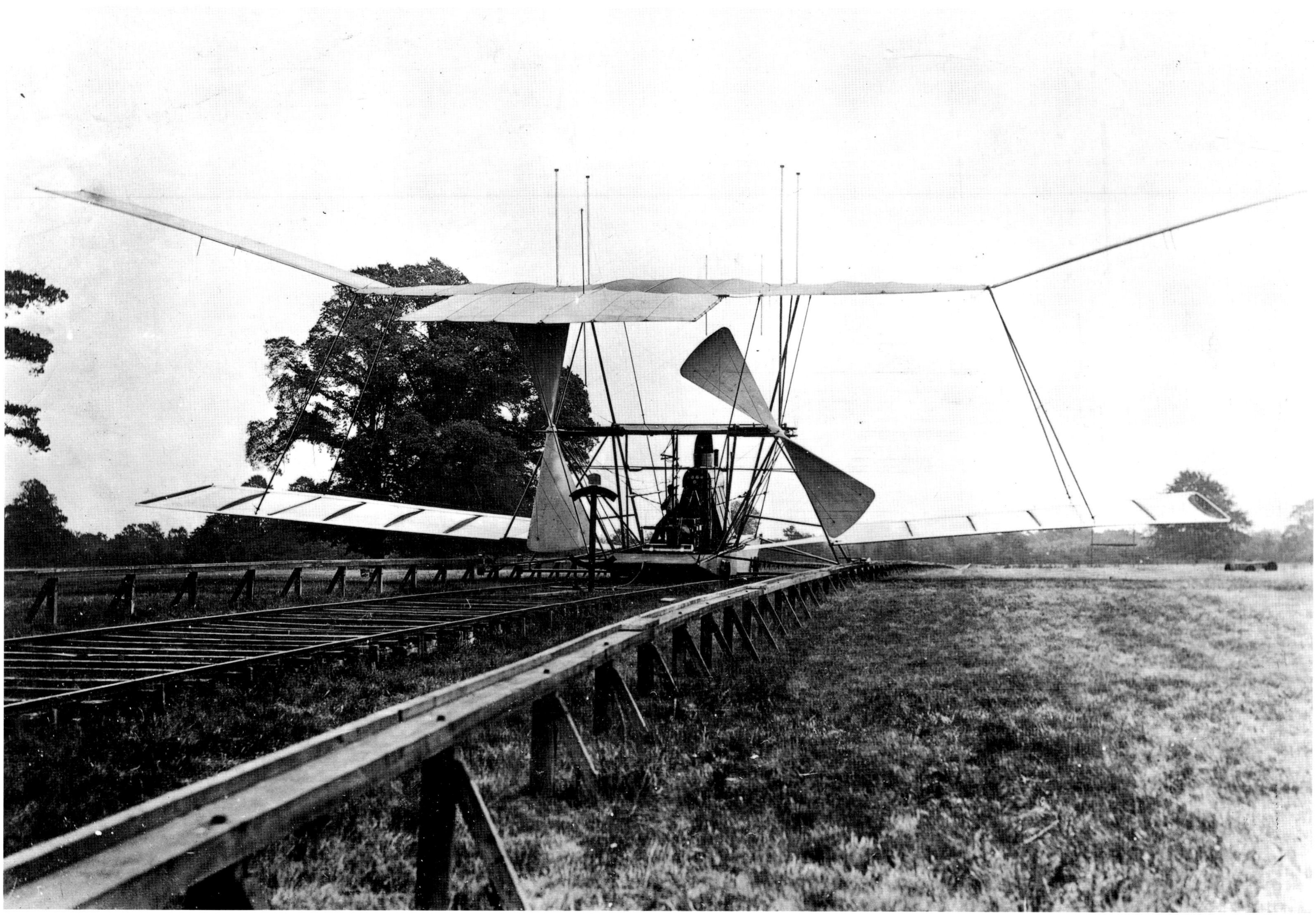

stability was the adoption of fixed horizontal control surfaces behind the wings, together with the abandonment of control surfaces forward of the wings. Although they made rapid and precise control possible, forward control surfaces could exert no weathercocking, or control on pitching motion by the aeroplane, and this emphasized longitudinal instability. Trailing control surfaces, however, had quite the reverse effect, while still allowing full longitudinal controllability. The man mainly responsible for this farsighted innovation, at least so far as biplanes were concerned, was Henry Farman. The Voisin-Farman I, in its many forms, had proved a sterling machine, but late in 1908 Farman decided that he needed a new model. Rather than commission a new one from the Voisins, he decided to try his hand at a design of his own. Despite his successes with the basic Voisin type, Farman produced an oddity, in the form of a tandem monoplane, which he designated the Farman II. He clearly had second thoughts about his machine, however, for it was abandoned even before completion. The designation was next transferred to a biplane commissioned by Farman from the Voisins, and paid for in advance.

It was this commission that produced one of the strangest and least explicable episodes in Gabriel Voisin's extraordinary career. Without informing anyone, he sold the pre-sold Voisin-Farman II to an Englishman, J.T.C. Brabazon, who had bought a standard Voisin the year before. Brabazon took his new machine back to England, where in April and May he made the first flights in the UK by a Briton. Despite the special modifications in the design demanded by Farman, the *Bird of Passage*, as the aeroplane was named by Brabazon, was not very successful and

crashed early in May. Quite naturally, Farman was disgusted by Gabriel Voisin's actions, but decided not to prosecute him. Instead he cut off all further contact with the Voisins, and decided to set up his own aircraft factory on the airfield at Camp de Châlons, south of Reims, where he had been flying since September 1908.

The first result of Farman's split with the Voisins was the Henry Farman III, destined to be one of the great aircraft of the period up to 1912. Three things are immediately apparent on this excellent machine. Firstly, Farman had moved away from the Voisin concept of total inherent lateral stability by means of dihedral and side-curtains, and had adopted four large ailerons for lateral control. This was the first time such surfaces had been incorporated in a fully practical fashion, and was an advance of considerable magnitude. Secondly, a stabilizing tailplane was added to the trailing fin and rudder assembly, although the Wright type of

forward elevator was still retained. Thirdly, the cumbersome, do-or-die appearance of earlier machines was replaced by an attractive, sturdy yet practical aspect that presaged the pusher biplanes of the next few years.

Powered by a 50-hp (37.3-kW) Vivinus engine driving a primitive Voisin propeller, the aeroplane was ready in April 1909. Farman quickly set about intensive flight trials, which soon proved the new machine's practicality. He realized that the area of the ailerons was excessive, and disconnected the pair on the lower wings, locking them in place as extensions of the flying surfaces. Shortly thereafter, Farman incorporated four smaller ailerons. In its

original form the Farman III was obsolete in one feature, namely its large cellular biplane tail. By August, Farman had modified this to an open configuration, and in this form the Farman III reached maturity as the progenitor of the classic European biplanes. Its best flight, on 19 July, lasted 1 hour 23 minutes, and so attractive was the type that two others were soon built for Roger Sommer and George Cockburn, putting Farman firmly on the scene as an aircraft manufacturer.

Despite their loss of Farman, the Voisins continued to prosper, building some 15 standard Voisins by the end of 1909. These were all conventional machines with few modifications, and

several made flights in excess of two hours' duration.

The Wrights continued to fly extensively in 1909, but with few modifications to their standard Model A machines. Those in service were mostly Dayton-built, but late in the year French-built examples started to reach their buyers. Meanwhile Orville Wright, now fully recovered from the crash that had killed Selfridge, restarted trials for the Signal Corps with a modified Model A featuring a smaller wing and taller landing gear skids. The tests had proved the satisfactory performance of the type by the end of July, and the American government bought the machine. Wilbur remained in

Europe, and continued to impress the crowds in France and Italy before returning to make demonstration flights in the USA from September to November. Wilbur's place in Europe was taken by Orville, who toured Germany in August, after the successful conclusion of the Signal Corps tests.

Levavasseur continued the work he had started with the Antoinette IV and V the year before with further revisions to these two types. The exact details are not catalogued, but most important of all was the alteration of the aileron system. In their 1908 forms, the Antoinette IV and V aircraft had been restricted to downward-operating ailerons only, whereby the aileron on the downward-moving wing remained floating, that on the other wing doing all the work. Levavasseur now realized the inefficiency of this, and provided differentially operating ailerons for 1909. On his next machine, the Antoinette VI, Levavasseur reverted to wing warping in place of the ailerons. This enhanced the natural beauty of the wings considerably, but to some it appears to have been a retrograde step. It should be remembered, however, that the long, narrow wing typical of the Antoinette monoplanes must have suffered considerably from torsional problems no matter how well braced they were, and it seems probable that Levavasseur decided to capitalize on this factor in using controlled torsion for lateral control. It is arguable, indeed, that the provision of large ailerons on so flexible a wing structure could be dangerous: the aileron could have operated as a servo-tab and twisted the wing to produce a bank opposite in effect to that desired.

The Antoinette VI was built for R. Demanest, but its performance was no

M. LOUIS BLÉRIOT.

M. BLÉRIOT'S AEROPLANE *on which he crossed the Channel from Calais to Dover, July 2*

The Blériot Type XI, on which the intrepid Louis Blériot first flew across the English Channel on 25 July 1909, defined the monoplane of its era and paved the way for the Blériot company's considerable commercial success. The wing was braced against flying and landing loads by wires from the landing gear and the cabane above the fuselage, warping of the wings' trailing edges was employed for lateral control, directional control was provided by the all-moving rudder, and longitudinal control was exercised by all-moving elevator segments at the tips of the tailplane.

more than average in its 15 flights between April and July 1909. Its successor was the Antoinette VII, the classic of the line, and was excelled in performance only by the redoubtable Antoinette IV. Built for Hubert Latham, a Frenchman of British parentage destined to play a vital role in the popularization of flying, the machine first flew on 27 July 1909. The Antoinette VIII, built for the firm and flown for the first time on 15 August, was also a beautiful machine, but it never performed with more than the modest of success.

In the monoplane field, 1909 was to be Blériot's year, despite the courageous and ill-fated efforts of Latham. What was to come was foreshadowed at the Salon de l'Automobile held at the end of 1908 in Paris. In the aviation section of this exhibition, Blériot displayed his two latest machines, the Blériot Nos IX and XI, which were all but completed. The former of these was ready for trials early in the new year, but proved abortive. The No. XI was an altogether more successful machine, and proved the foundation of Blériot's success as an aircraft constructor. In its original form, the No. XI looked very odd. This was a result of the stabilizing fin mounted on pylons above the pilot's head, near the front of the fuselage. Controls were the now conventional warping, rear elevator and rudder. The No. XI was ready toward the

end of January 1909, but two months of effort produced nothing better than one two-minute flight early in April. Blériot belatedly realized that modifications were in order and a further two months passed while the No. XI was transformed into the No. XI (Modified). The central forward fin was deleted, the rear rudder was enlarged, and, most important of all, an efficient Chauvière propeller was fitted to the 25-hp (18.6-kW) Anzani arrowhead engine which replaced the earlier 30-hp (22.4-kW) REP unit. Results were immediately impressive, principally as a result of the far greater thrust provided by the Chauvière propeller. Blériot made some excellent duration and cross-country flights in this machine before turning his attention towards the English Channel. It should be noted additionally that the No. XI was the first European aeroplane to utilize the Wright type of wing warping absolutely successfully.

In the spring of 1909, Blériot also determined to be the first man in history to produce a truly adequate passenger-carrying aeroplane. Accordingly he set to work and in May unveiled the No. XII. This was essentially a scaled-up standard Blériot type, powered at first by a 35-hp (26.1-kW) ENV engine, and later by a 60-hp (44.7-kW) unit from the same manufacturer. Provision was made for one passenger and the pilot, although Blériot carried two passengers to win a special prize at the Reims aviation meeting in August. The No. XIII was basically similar to its predecessor, but was powered by a 40-hp (29.8-kW) Anzani instead of being powered by an ENV.

Although unsuccessful in relative terms, two designs of this year were to have a profound influence on the future development of tractor biplanes. These were the Goupy II and Bréguet I. The Goupy, designed by Ambroise Goupy and Mario Calderera but built by Blériot, was an advanced design, with a staggered wing cellule (the top wing being ahead of the lower wing) on a fuselage and empennage based on Blériot's designs. At first it was not successful, but with wing-tip elevons it started a useful career as a school aeroplane from the end of 1909. The Bréguet, designed and built by Louis Bréguet, was not as advanced in appearance as the Goupy II, but it played a more prominent part in the development of tractor biplanes. It was shown at the Aeronautical Show held at Olympia in London in March 1909, and was ready for flight in June. The one very unusual feature of the machine was the double use of warping: in concert as elevators and differentially as ailerons. Unlike the Goupy II, the Bréguet I took part in the Reims aviation meeting where its distinctive and prophetic lines gave rise to much comment.

The UK was only now beginning to emerge from the aeronautical doldrums. Two men were principally responsible for this, and one of them, the American Samuel Franklin Cody, was not yet a British citizen. After the hesitant and minor successes of his first powered aeroplane, known as the British Army Aeroplane No. 1, Cody in the last quarter of 1908 rebuilt his machine into what may be termed the Cody 2, which made some 30 flights in the first half of 1909, the best of them covering 4 miles (6.4km). Subsequent modification turned this machine into the Cody 3, on which the magnificent Cody achieved several successful flights, the best of them covering 40 miles (64km) in just over 60 minutes on 8 September 1909. These Cody machines were large, sturdy, but clumsy

machines, and exerted no real influence on the mainstream of aviation. They were, however, important in showing the British people that aircraft could fly, and that one designed in their own country, even if not by one of their own countrymen, could remain in the air for a considerable period. Cody's enthusiasm and determination were an encouragement to all would-be British pioneers, and helped alleviate the unconscious British fears that the Continentals had stolen a march on them.

The only other British pioneer of the period to achieve anything like success was Alliot Verdon Roe with a series of triplanes inspired by the unsuccessful Goupy I. Roe was acutely short of money, however, and at first could afford nothing better as powerplants than the 6- and 9-hp (4.5- and 6.7-kW) JAP engines, with which he could achieve nothing better than powered hops in his otherwise promising machines.

In the USA, Curtiss started his own aircraft business in conjunction with Augustus Herring, Chanute's associate of 10 years earlier, at the beginning of 1909. The firm's first machine, built for the Aeronautic Society of New York but soon lent to Curtiss, was the *Gold Bug*. Like the *Silver Wing*, this machine evolved from the *June Bug* and continued the basic design philosophy of the AEA, but it had parallel wings instead of the dihedral/anhedral curved wings favoured by AEA types. Powerful ailerons were installed at mid-gap, but otherwise the aeroplane was conventional by the standards of the day. The *Gold Bug* was making successful flights by the late spring of 1909, but by then Curtiss had decided to build a machine for himself, principally as a racing machine and record-breaker. He had clearly foreseen that public enthusiasm for aviation would soon begin to pour hard cash into the

sport, and that considerable sums could be secured by the first man to develop a specialized aircraft. The *Golden Flyer*, as Curtiss' machine was called, was similar in layout to the *Gold Bug*, but was powered by a new 50-hp (37.3-kW) Curtiss engine, although for tactical reasons Curtiss often stated that the engine could deliver only 30hp (22.4kW). The *Golden Flyer* was ready just in time for the Reims aviation meeting, and exerted a powerful influence on other designers following its great successes there.

Two events of 1909 finally put aviation right in the public eye. Aviation, up until that year, had been considered a kind of madcap sport to be indulged in by wealthy or eccentric men with little better to do. No practical application for what had become a practical activity was envisaged by any but the most far-sighted. Then, in July 1909, Blériot succeeded in flying across the English Channel from France to England. The shock of this singular event was out of all proportion to the flight's significance as such, and its ripples reached out over Europe, the USA and the British Empire. For the first time people realized that a new way of life was about to break on them. The inviolability of the British Isles through its mighty navy was seen to be suddenly challenged, as there now existed in rudimentary form the means of circumventing the Royal Navy's supremacy. The Channel flight ensured Blériot's financial success as an aircraft constructor, to add to his success as a motor car manufacturer, for within two days he had received orders for over 100 Blériot XI aircraft.

The other major event of 1909 was La Grande Semaine d'Aviation de la Champagne (Champagne great aviation week), the first great flying meeting to be

held. This grand affair attracted all the best pilots and machines in Europe, and was held on the open spaces near Bétheny outside Reims between 22 and 29 August. With many generous prizes offered by the champagne industry, the meeting was attended by many influential political and financial figures from all over Europe. It may truly be said that this meeting, with its plethora of events, flights and records, marked the beginning of Europe's acceptance of the aeroplane as more than just a toy.

It would be tedious to list all the events and successes of the meeting and the barest statistics must suffice to show how major an event that week was. There were 38 entries, of which only 23 succeeded in taking off. Of the 120 take-offs they made, 87 resulted in flights of over 3.1 miles (5km) and seven of over 62 miles (100km). The best flight recorded was by Henry Farman in his Farman III, now powered by the new 50-hp (37.3-kW) Gnome rotary engine, with a flight of 112 miles (180km) in just over three hours. Curtiss took the speed prize at 46.6mph (75km/h) with his *Golden Flyer*, and Latham took the altitude prize with a height of 508ft (155m) in the Antoinette VII. There were four other prizes for heavier-than-air craft, and two for lighter-than-air craft. The highest speed recorded at the event, though not during the competition for the speed prize, was in the special short sprint race, won by Blériot on his No. XII at a speed of 47.8mph (76.95km/h).

The meeting was a great success from every aspect, and set the style for similar events all over Europe in the next few years.

Chapter Four
Faster & Higher

Flying was now becoming international, and nowhere was this more apparent than in the expanding number of races and competitions that took place. This internationalism lay not only in the number of places where the competitions were held, but also in the nationalities of the competitors themselves. Although most of them flew French aircraft, an increasing number of British machines was evident, marking the formal arrival of the UK onto the aeronautical scene.

Despite the paucity of American pilots and designers, entrepreneurs in the USA were quick to realize the draw of flying, and in January 1910 the first international competition to take place in that country was held in Los Angeles. Honours were shared between France and the USA: Louis Paulhan in a Henry Farman set a world altitude record at 4,165ft (1269.5m) and Curtiss established a world speed record at 55mph (88.5km/h) with a machine of his own design. Attendances were very large, and promoters in other cities were suddenly aware that aviation was a real money-spinner. In September there was a highly successful meeting in Boston, where most of the competitors were American and British, and the lively and dynamic figure of Claude Grahame-White dominated

proceedings. Most of these competitors then moved south to New York for the meeting arranged for October in Belmont Park, again dominated by Grahame-White, who had caused a great stir by flying down to Washington before the meeting and landing in the street outside the White House to pay his respects to President Taft. America was now firmly in the grip of the flying bug and races proliferated. So too did daredevil flying, or barnstorming as it came to be called, and record attempts.

The explosion of interest in flight after Reims was not confined to the USA. During 1910 meetings were held all over Europe: four in Italy, two in Germany, one each in Spain, Switzerland, Belgium, Denmark, Russia and Hungary, and many in the UK and France. Crowds continued to flock to the displays and races, which steadily increased in size during the next few years. They were usually held close to large cities, sometimes on specially hired grounds and sometimes on airfields specially bought and built up by a few enterprising promoters such as Grahame-White, whose establishment of Hendon as one of the major flying areas for London is a very good example. Flying displays became a regular feature of weekend life in the cities of Europe, attended alike by

the aristocracy, the middle classes and the mass of working people who could get to the field. All were catered for in separate enclosures, and large fortunes were made by the entrepreneurs who were lucky enough to have their preparations and enterprise attended by good weather.

The prize money available to constructors at air displays was of course added to by that put up for special races. These included the Trans-America race, the London-Manchester race for a prize of £10,000 put up by the *Daily Mail* and won by Paulhan in April 1910 flying a Henry Farman, the 1911 Circuit of Britain race for the *Daily Mail* prize of £10,000 won by André Beaumont, the 1911 Circuit of Europe race for £18,300 also won by Beaumont, the French Michelin races for distance flown with an annual prize of 20,000 francs, and the British Empire Michelin Cup races each worth £500, which were also annual races for distance flown. By the standards of the day these were very valuable prizes, and winning them made a considerable difference to the finances of most designers and constructors.

The number of constructors had grown considerably, and large companies with other basic interests were now taking an increasing share of the market. The

best companies, however, were those that had got off to a sound start with aircraft that could fly in 1908 and 1909. When their own types were not selling very successfully, these companies could always undertake the building of a one-off design, or the licence-production of aircraft whose output could not keep up with demand. By 1914, therefore, the building of aircraft was in the hands of a number of small builders, producing only a few aircraft a year, and a few larger companies capable of turning out far more machines such as Bristol, Short Brothers, Blériot, Morane-Saulnier, Albatros and Caproni. These companies were to bear the brunt of the production race in the opening months of the war.

People who would never be able to afford aircraft of their own could now take part in the adventure of flight by being passengers. One or two passengers had already been carried on a variety of aircraft when Claude Grahame-White, who always seemed to be a couple of jumps ahead of the rest of the field when assessing the future of aviation, decided that passenger flights should be added to the attractions of his displays and school at Hendon. The result was his extraordinary *Charabanc*, which flew for the first time late in the summer of 1913.

With its circular-section monocoque (single-shell) fuselage of wooden construction and neatly cowled rotary engine driving a propeller fitted with a drag-reducing spinner, the Deperdussin Monocoque racing aeroplane was the last word for aerodynamic cleanliness in the period before World War I.

On 2 October the type established a new world record by taking off with nine passengers and staying in the air for just under 20 minutes. On 11 February 1914 this record was bettered by the Sikorsky *Le Grand*, which took 16 people up. This odd four-engined machine, which soon evolved into the world's first four-engined bomber, even had a promenade deck along the upper rear fuselage, with rails to prevent passengers falling off as the huge machine lumbered along!

But while these aircraft were amusing the audience at air displays, and while adventurous pilots were pushing forward the limits of their steadily improving machines, aircraft were gradually embroiled in warfare for the first time. The tinge of excitement felt by the spectator on the ground during an air display, watching for the half-expected misfortune to an aeroplane going through its manoeuvres, was starting its long transformation into the terror of the

bomber's approach during World War II.

Uncertain as they were of the role aircraft could play in war, governments were at first hesitant to spend lavishly on the formation of air services. But the British army had used balloons regularly since 1878, and in 1907 the German army had established its airship service. It was inevitable that properly organized air services would be raised shortly after the Reims meeting had proved the practicality of aircraft to the European authorities,

both civilian and military. The USA had already paved the way with the purchase of a Wright biplane, named *Miss Columbia*, for $30,000 on 2 August 1909. In 1910 France, Germany and Russia all established air services for their armies, although the German service was not formally established until October 1912. The UK followed suit in April 1911 with the formation of the Air Battalion, Royal Engineers, expanded into the Royal Flying Corps, with Military and Naval Wings, in May 1912. In July 1914 this was split as the Royal Navy established its own Royal Naval Air Service.

The first use of aircraft in war, however, was not by one of these formally established bodies, but by the Italians, who still lacked a proper air service. The Italian army fighting the Turks in Libya used a number of aircraft provided by the Royal Aero Club of Italy, and history was made on 22 October 1911 when Captain Piazza carried out the first air reconnaissance of Turkish positions near Aziziya in a Blériot. On 1 November further history was made when Lieutenant Gavotti dropped four home-made bombs on a Turkish camp from his Etrich Taube. The Turks immediately claimed that this constituted a war crime because a hospital had been hit, although this seems unlikely. On 24 November Captain Moizo carried out the first artillery spotter flight, and on 23 February 1913 Piazza flew the world's first photographic-reconnaissance mission. Thus were born the four basic tasks to be fulfilled by aircraft in World War I. The Italians had been sufficiently impressed by the results gained by aircraft that they set up an army air service in June 1912. Further military uses for aircraft were discovered during the Balkan Wars of 1912–1913.

Other European interest in the military applications of aircraft continued in 1911 and 1912, even if it was only in a desultory fashion. In October and November of 1911 the French held the first military aircraft competition, or Concours Militaire, to find aircraft types suitable for the army air service, and experiments with armament, both bombs and machine-guns, were carried out. The first few aircraft specifically intended for war, including a two-seater Nieuport equipped with a machine-gun, also appeared.

In 1912, for the first time, armies began to consider seriously what to do with their aircraft, and thus what sort of aircraft they should have. This was partially the result of their own internal considerations, but also a result of the increasing insistence of the public. Although the authorities showed little interest, several interesting British designs were emerging. Roe had led the way in the development of the fully practical tractor biplane with the Avro Types D and E of 1911 and the Type F of 1912, culminating in the great Avro Type 504 of 1913. Geoffrey de Havilland, working at the Royal Aircraft Factory at Farnborough, had evolved the fully stable

B.E.2 from the partially successful B.E.1 of the previous year. Most importantly, however, de Havilland had produced the B.S.1 as a fast, clean tractor biplane, the machine from which all fighters may trace their descent. But at the British Military Aircraft Competition held in August 1912, the B.E.2, as a government-sponsored machine, was not allowed to compete against private-enterprise aircraft, and Cody's extraordinary Military Trials Biplane was declared the winner, although the B.E.2, flying *hors de concours*, was manifestly superior. Only two of the Cody machines were ordered for the Royal Flying Corps, however, and the inherently stable B.E.2 was put into production.

Although the development and introduction of a number of standard

types, such as the B.E.2 and imported Blériot No. XI, as well as a variety of Avro and Sopwith types, dominated the thinking of those concerned with British military aviation in the last two years before the outbreak of World War I, there were other factors that were in the long-term of greater significance. Eugene Ely in the USA had made the first take-off and landing aboard ship, but it was the British who in many respects took the lead in the operation of wheeled aircraft from ships with a number of take-offs from the pre-Dreadnought battleships *London* and *Hibernia* while the ships were under way. Thus although Ely's feats had been considerable firsts, the British efforts paved the way for everyday operations from moving warships, and also opened

up the possibility of warships designed specifically to operate aircraft at sea.

Unfortunately for aviation, 1912 had seen the partial eclipse of the monoplane. This was the result of two crashes in England, and of Blériot's doubts about the structural integrity of his basic layout. Both the British and French armies had immediately placed a ban on the monoplane layout, and although the ban was subsequently lifted, it took monoplanes some 20 years to come back into favour.

Among the most important design advances of 1913 were the full development of the B.E.2, and the introduction of the lovely little Sopwith Tabloid side-by-side two-seater designed by Harry Hawker and Fred Sigrist. In France the fastest aircraft of the pre-war period made its appearance. This was the Deperdussin Monocoque, a beautifully streamlined monoplane capable of 126mph (203km/h, which looked forward to the racing aircraft of the 1920s with its monocoque (stressed single-shell) fuselage, enclosed engine and careful

ABOVE
Seen here in the cockpit of the Deperdussin Monocoque, Maurice Prévost of France was one of the great racing and exhibition pilots of the first decade of powered flight, and would today be regarded as a test pilot as much as a stunt flier.

OPPOSITE
Maurice Prévost in the 1913 Deperdussin Monocoque rounds one of the corner markers for that year's Gordon Bennett Trophy race, revealing impeccable piloting technique in his banked and slightly diving turn to ensure no appreciable loss of speed.

attention to the elimination of drag-producing factors.

The events of 1913, however, were notable not so much for the emergence of new types of aircraft as for the rapid development of the art of flying, and of the science of designing and building aircraft. Aerobatics came into their own, partially because there was a market for them, and daring pilots were prepared to risk their necks to exploit it, but also because thought and experimentation had led to a closer understanding of the forces acting upon an aircraft in flight. Combined with sturdier airframes and reliable engines, this enabled daring pilots to try aerobatics with some degree of safety. There were, of course, accidents, but it was only because of the activities of pilots such as Pégoud that flying advanced rapidly past the chauffeur attitude towards full mastery of the air.

The advances made in the years before the world plunged into war are best made clear through a few statistics. Since 1909, the world speed record had improved from 47.85mph (77km/h) to 126.67mph (203.86km/h), the range record had risen from 145.59 miles (234.3km) to 634.54 miles (1021.23km) and the altitude record had increased from 1,486ft (452.9m) to 20,079ft (6120m). But these advances were about to be utterly outstripped as aviation in the next few years would receive its most profound, if perhaps regrettable, stimulus.

Chapter Five

World War I –
The Birth of Military Aviation

The widespread use of aircraft in World War I inevitably altered both the nature of aviation and public opinion about flight and fliers. Although aircraft had seen limited use as military weapons in the last few years before World War I, in 1914 most Europeans still considered flight to be the province of adventurous spirits who flew for sport and for excitement, without any real practical purpose. But by the end of the conflict aviation was very big business. Many thousands of aircraft and engines had been built in a multitude of factories, most of which had no connection with aviation before the start of hostilities in August 1914. The air forces of the combatant nations, too, had grown into potent weapons of war, revealing to the far-sighted the potential that in World War II was to usher in the era of total war in which every man, woman and child, no matter how remote from the actual fighting front, was liable to attack.

Yet when the war started few foresaw what was about to happen, for the role of aircraft was still uncertain. Although experiments with armament, principally light machine-guns and small bombs, had been carried out before the war, general military enthusiasm for the concept of armed aircraft had been lukewarm at best.

But despite military authorities' refusal to study the benefits and disadvantages of aircraft with any insight, enthusiasts called for aircraft to take their place in the nations' armed forces. This pressure, combined with a desire not to allow any one country to take a lead in building an air force, eventually led the French,

LEFT
In June 1912 the US Army began trials of a machine-gun mounted in an aeroplane. Captain Charles de Forest Chandler is here manning a Lewis air-cooled gun somewhat casually mounted on a Wright Model B biplane. Stripped of its cumbersome air-cooling jacket, the Lewis gun was the standard trainable weapon of Allied aircraft in World War I.

OPPOSITE
Typical of the mettlesome aviators who became the first air aces of World War I was Jean Navarre of France, who had been a pre-war pilot, scored his first victory on 1 April 1915 with a rifle, and then scored another 11 kills before suffering a mental breakdown in June 1916. He returned to flying late in 1918 but was killed in a crash during July 1919, eight months after the end of World War I.

German, British and other European governments to sanction the introduction of aircraft into their military forces. Both France and Germany, the latter spurred on by the public air-mindedness engendered by the success of Ferdinand, Graf von Zeppelin's great airships and the Kaiser's desire that his country be not outstripped in any technical way by France, soon led the field. Public indignation at this at last forced the British Government to spend more generously on their forces, and in 1913 more that £1,000,000 was allocated for the first time.

Thus the armed forces now had aircraft. But what were they to do with them? How best were the services to exploit these expensive machines and the equally expensive force of men to fly and maintain them? The only possible solution in the years immediately preceding World War I seemed to be reconnaissance of two types: firstly tactical or strategic reconnaissance for commanders, and secondly spotting for the artillery. In the former, it was hoped, a trained officer would be able to use the vantage point the aircraft gave him to observe and note down enemy dispositions and movements and then report them to his command. In the latter an officer could spot the fall of his battery's shot, and then issue corrections which could be delivered in a weighted container, by signalling with manoeuvres or, it was hoped, by radio once a suitably light transmitter had been developed. France and Germany, both of whom placed great reliance on artillery, were quick to adopt the role of artillery spotting for their air forces. The UK still lagged behind technically and theoretically, however, despite the efforts of many junior officers, and until 1914 its

air forces were seen as an unwanted supplement to the cavalry in the latter's traditional capacity as light reconnoitring forces.

The various military aircraft competitions held in 1911 and 1912 had been intended to produce types that could be standardized for the squadrons, thus easing procurement and maintenance problems. Yet it was one thing to select what was considered a type suitable for widespread use, and another to get it into mass-production and thus into widespread service. The aviation industry of the period was just not geared to mass-production: most factories had experience only in the building of one-off types for designers or in very limited production. The result, in military terms, was that chosen designs could not as yet be built in sufficient quantity and there could be little standardization of types within the squadrons. In this respect the Germans and French were better off than the British. The Germans fielded a large number of Taube (dove) types derived from the experiments of Etrich and Wels, as well as units homogeneously equipped with tractor biplanes of Albatros and Aviatik design. The French had squadrons of Voisin biplane bombers, and Blériot and Morane-Saulnier monoplanes for reconnaissance work. The British, almost inevitably, went to war with several French aircraft plus a large miscellany of British types, the best of which were the Royal Aircraft Factory's Blériot Experimental (B.E.) 2, the Sopwith Tabloid, the Bristol Scout D and various marks of Avro Type 504. It is worth noting here that an odd system of nomenclature was used for Royal Aircraft Factory types. Forbidden to build aircraft so that it should not come into financial

competition with the private aircraft industry, the factory resorted to a splendid ruse: allowed to repair damaged Royal Flying Corps machines, it in fact produced new types and claimed that these were merely extensive rebuilds and modifications of machines too severely damaged for conventional repair. The factory then produced a number of designs with prefixes such as B.E., F.E. (Farman Experimental), S.E. (Scouting Experimental) and R.E. (Reconnaissance Experimental). Eventually the factory got permission to build types, but by then the designations were so accepted that they were retained. Even after it had been allowed to build its designs, however, the factory's production capacity remained small, with the result that most Royal Aircraft Factory designs were built by private concerns under contract to the government.

During the first stages of the war when it finally broke out, the Allied powers operated 233 aircraft (160 French and 73 British in France) against the Germans' total of 246. At first the weather was superb, but the aircraft had not been designed for intensive operations and their serviceability was low, a factor compounded by the number of different types and engines in service at a time when the Allies were in full retreat and all logistical backing was run on an extemporized basis.

Although their primary tasks were reconnaissance and artillery spotting when the front was stable, the young and adventurous pilots of the day saw no reason why both sides should enjoy such benefits, when it might be possible to prevent the enemy from acquiring information by the apparently simple expedient of shooting at him and perhaps forcing him down. It was not long, therefore, before the first weapons made their appearance in the air. Initially these weapons consisted of personal equipment such as rifles and pistols. The resultant aerial duels stood little chance of inflicting mortal damage on either of the parties. More hopeful, or perhaps just less realistic, innovators tried shotguns, hand grenades, bricks and even grappling hooks on the end of lengths of cord, the last of which it was hoped would hit and destroy the enemy's propeller. Others again decided that zooming close to the enemy might cause the pilot's nerve to fail and so cause him to come down.

It was only a matter of time before effective aerial armament began to take effect, and on 5 October 1914 a French gunner, Caporal Quénault, shot down an Aviatik two-seater with the Hotchkiss machine-gun mounted in the front of the nacelle of a Voisin bomber flown by Sergeant Joseph Frantz. From this time

onwards the incidence of aerial combats, and also of aerial victories, began slowly to climb. But there remained one basic problem to be solved before air combat could reach a large scale, and this factor of interference between gun and propeller was not to be solved until 1915.

It had also occurred to various pilots early in the history of aviation that if one could fly over a target, then one could also drop missiles on it, and early in the war practical work on the development of bombing got under way. As early as 30 June 1910 the indefatigable Glenn Curtiss

had dropped dummy bombs on the outline of a battleship buoyed out on Lake Keuka, New York. Bombing competitions, using bags of flour, had even become a popular feature of pre-war flying meetings.

The French and Germans, particularly the former, were concerned with bombing from the beginning of the war. On 14 August the French sent two Voisins to attack the Zeppelin sheds at Metz-Frascaty, and on 30 August a German Taube dropped five small bombs on Paris, killing one civilian and injuring another two. The Royal Flying Corps (RFC) was not at first

especially interested in bombing, but its naval sister service, the Royal Naval Air Service, showed more enterprise, launching its first, and in the event abortive, raid on the Zeppelin sheds at Düsseldorf with two aircraft from Antwerp on 22 September. Another raid on the same target was launched on 8 October, and this time the Zeppelin Z.IX was destroyed.

The problem that had hindered the development of true air fighting, that of the location of the machine-gun relative to the propeller, was easily solved on the older, pusher type of two-seaters. A light

LEFT
The introduction of an effective synchronization system for the Vickers machine-gun and the creation of sturdy yet highly manoeuvrable fighters such as the Sopwith Camel paved the way for Allied aces such as Raymond Collishaw, who was of Canadian birth but flew for the Royal Naval Air Service and Royal Air Force in a career that saw 60 victories to put Collishaw third on the list of British aces.

OPPOSITE
Early Nieuport fighters, such as this Nie.12 with an overwing Lewis gun, were of the sesquiplane configuration with a lower wing much smaller than the upper wing. Possessing only a single spar, the lower wing was prone to twisting in high-speed dives and hard manoeuvring, and sometimes broke away.

machine-gun, usually on a simple pillar mounting to allow easy traverse and elevation, was mounted at the front of the nacelle for the observer's use. Even on the newer tractor two-seaters, though the results were not particularly good, the observer could be provided with a light machine-gun capable of upward, rearward and lateral fire. The disadvantage of this latter system, however, was that the observer usually occupied the forward of the two seats so that the removal of his weight, on or near the aeroplane's centre of gravity, would not affect the trim of

the machine on solo flights. This meant that the observer was located between the wings, which seriously curtailed his field of vision and of fire, surrounded as he was by a mass of rigging and bracing wires, many of which would be cut by bullets. The matter was later reconsidered and improved by reversing the positions of pilot and observer so that the observer had an improved field of fire over the aircraft's rear.

But although armament could be and was fitted to two-seaters from the earliest days of the war, two-seaters were not

really suited to conversion into fighters, or scouts, as such aircraft were then designated. The two-seaters were too big, heavy, clumsy and slow. What was needed was a single-seater fighter, but tractor types were almost universal by 1915 and the problem of the position of the gun relative to the propeller became very difficult. The only practical solution to the sighting problem was to fix the gun along the aircraft's centreline, so that basically all the pilot had to do was aim his whole machine at the target and press the trigger. What was needed was a

method of stopping the occasional bullet from striking the propeller blades. Experiments carried out before the war by Franz Schneider of the German LVG concern and Raymond Saulnier of the French Morane-Saulnier company had paved the way, with the invention of primitive interrupter gears which halted the action of the gun when there was a propeller blade in front of the muzzle. But both experimenters' efforts had foundered on the problem of hang-fire rounds. Here the fault lay with the manufacture of the primer and propellant for the ammunition: inconsistencies in the chemical compounds meant that occasionally bullets fired fractionally later than they should, obviating the work of the interrupter and shattering a blade. To preserve these expensive items, Saulnier had fitted the propellers he used for experiments with special steel deflectors, wedge-shaped items bolted to the back of the propeller blades in line with the gun to deflect any bullet that was heading for a blade. The advent of war had curtailed these experiments in favour of immediate production.

Early in 1915 the idea was resurrected by Saulnier and the great pre-war stunt pilot Roland Garros, now serving with the French Aviation Militaire. Probably at the instigation of the headstrong Garros, it was soon decided by the two men that the actual interrupter gear should be omitted for the sake of lightness and simplicity, the few bullets that would hit a blade being warded off by the deflectors. Preliminary tests proved successful, and in March 1915 Garros returned to his unit with his modified Morane-Saulnier Type L parasol-wing scout. All was ready on 1 April 1915 and Garros set off in search of prey. He soon ran into four German Albatros two-seaters, which displayed no signs of fear or evasive action as the French scout closed in head-on, conventionally a safe angle. Then all of a sudden a stream of bullets flew out from the nose of the Type L and an Albatros plummeted down, its pilot dead at the controls. Before the astounded Germans could react, Garros had turned and fired at another Albatros, which immediately burst into flames and crashed. The remaining two Albatroses immediately fled, taking with them the first news of the arrival of the era of the true fighter aeroplane.

In the next 17 days Garros managed to bag another three aircraft, thus becoming the world's first ace fighter pilot. Although the Germans were mystified by this French success, the secret was soon to fall into their hands:

on 19 April Garros was forced down behind the German lines as the result of an inevitable engine failure. In the course of almost three weeks of combat, the propeller blades of his aeroplane had been shaken many times as the deflectors forced away bullets, the consequent vibration being transmitted via the crankshaft to the already highly stressed 80-hp (59.6-kW) rotary engine. Some form of engine failure had to happen, and Garros was unlucky that the prevailing westerly wind gave him no chance of gliding back over the lines. He was captured before he could set fire to his aeroplane. The capture of this remarkable French aeroplane was a welcome surprise to the Germans, who immediately ordered Anthony Fokker, the enigmatic Dutch designer working for them, to copy the system on his M 5 Eindecker (monoplane) just introduced. Fokker entrusted the task to his design team, and in 48 hours this able group of men had

produced an efficient interrupter gear for the 7.92-mm (0.312-in) LMG 14 Parabellum machine-gun then in widespread use as the standard German aerial gun. (The LMG 14 was soon supplanted as the standard fixed gun by the 7.92-mm/0.312-in MG 08/15 machine-gun made at Spandau near Berlin, hence the popular Allied misnomer of the gun as the Spandau.) The Fokker interrupter, which was tested on an M 5k monoplane, redesignated E I when it entered service with armament,

was very simple but effective. Improved models were the E II and E III, which were the main instruments of the Fokker scourge that now began.

The Fokker monoplanes ruled supreme in the autumn and winter of 1915, with the Allies apparently loath to copy the German interrupter gear. But at last, in the spring of 1916, the Allies began to make headway, albeit still without an interrupter gear. The French produced the delightful Nieuport Nie.11 Bébé (baby) sesquiplane, with a Lewis

gun firing over the top wing to clear the upper arc of the disc swept by the propeller. The British introduced the Airco (de Havilland) D.H.2, a neat pusher biplane with a Lewis gun mounted at the front of the one-man nacelle. These two types gradually wrested command of the air from the Germans, first allowing their own two-seaters to work more effectively against the German land forces, and their taking the air war effectively to the Germans, driving the latters' observation machines virtually from the

air. The Fokker Scourge was defeated by April, and the Allies quickly exploited their command of the air by pushing several new types into action in the second half of the year. At least interrupter gears were making a widespread appearance on the Allied side on such excellent types as the Nieuport Nie.17 and SPAD S.7, both French, and the British Sopwith 1 1/2-Strutter and Sopwith Pup. All four aircraft were fitted with one 0.303-in (7.7-mm) Vickers fixed forward-firing gun, and the 1 1/2-Strutter, so named for its single sets of interplane struts and half struts supporting the centre section, also had a Lewis gun for the observer.

Toward the end of 1916 the inexorable see-saw of technology over the front had swung the balance in favour of Germany once again. Realizing that the Allies would produce a counter to the Eindecker by the middle of 1916, the Germans had set about developing a new generation of aircraft late in 1915. At the heart of this resurgence in German air strength was the series of Albatros single-seat fighters, starting with the D I, D II and D III, the last of which entered

LEFT
Combining strength, performance, agility and two-gun armament (normally two Vickers guns on the upper part of the fuselage in a humped fairing that led to the type's nickname), the Sopwith Camel was the most successful British fighter of World War I, but was a tricky machine to fly.

OPPOSITE
Basically an improved development of the Camel, the Sopwith Snipe entered service late in World War I and was flown in a number of classic engagements.

service early in 1917. These sleek, shark-like biplanes with their plywood fuselages and well-cowled engines were capable of very good performance. Most importantly of all, however, they were armed with two machine-guns, and in the spring of 1917 this gave them twice the firepower of Allied types. The immediate consequence of the arrival of these new German fighters was total command of the air, and what became known in the RFC as Bloody April, when the British suffered losses in aircrews and aircraft of some 30 per cent, their highest losses of the entire war.

The second quarter of 1917 found both sides exhausted by Bloody April, the only success of which had been, from the British point of view, the handful of Sopwith Triplane fighters. Although armed with only one machine-gun, this was a clean aeroplane that could combat the Albatrosses by means of its remarkable rate of climb and general agility, both functions of the large wing area contained within the small overall dimensions of a triplane layout. So impressed were the Germans that orders for triplane designs were immediately issued. The type ordered into production was the Fokker

Dr I, the aeroplane flown by Baron von Richthofen at the time of his death. Although very manoeuvrable, the Dr I in fact appeared after the epoch of the triplane, and lacked the performance to make it a fighter suitable for any but the most experienced of pilots.

Yet there was some hope on the horizon for the Allies during Bloody April in the form of new aircraft types. First to arrive, late in April, was the Royal Aircraft Factory S.E.5. This, and its higher-powered S.E.5a variant, introduced two-gun armament to Allied fighters and thus equalled the firepower of German types,

at the same time improving upon their performance. The ruggedness and steadiness of the S.E.5, which did not have the inherent stability of the B.E.2 series, made it an excellent combat type, probably the best gun platform of the war. Oddly enough, at a time when other two-gun types were appearing with twin Vickers interrupted guns, the S.E.5/5a had only a single Vickers gun in the forward fuselage, the other gun being an uninterrupted Lewis firing over the top wing. Late in May the S.E.5 was joined by the French SPAD S.13, an improved version of the S.7 with more power and two guns. Fast and rugged, the S.13 was the best French fighter of the war, and was also used extensively by the Italians and Americans.

Both the S.E.5 and S.13 were fitted with powerful Vee engines, but the third new Allied fighter that brought about the eclipse of the German air force in the middle of 1917 was the ultimate expression of the classic rotary-engined design philosophy. This was the Sopwith Camel, which appeared in July 1917.

OPPOSITE

The Fokker D VIII parasol-wing fighter was used in modest numbers late in World War I and secured moderately good performance from the combination of an indifferent engine with a very clean airframe. This later was the work of Reinhold Platz, who went on to create the great Fokker warplanes and transports of the 1920s, and combined a thick-section cantilever wing of plywood-covered wooden construction with a fuselage and tail unit of fabric-covered welded steel tube construction.

RIGHT

The standard defensive armament of two-seaters such as this Bréguet Bre.14 late in World War I, was a pair of Lewis guns on a Scarff ring mounting.

Bearing a strong resemblance to the Pup, the Camel lacked the earlier type's lightness of appearance, featuring instead a slightly squat, pugnacious belligerence emphasized by the hump over the breeches of the twin Vickers guns that led to the type's nickname, later officially adopted. With the propeller, engine, fuel, oil, guns, ammunition and pilot all squeezed into the front 7ft (2.13m) of the fuselage, where their inertia would least interfere with manoeuvrability, the Camel was supremely agile. The fourth fighter to end German dominance of the air, a role it played for the rest of the war, was the Bristol F.2B Fighter which entered service in the summer of 1917. Originally intended as a standard two-seater to supplement the RFC's F.K.8 and R.E.8 machines, the F.2A version of the aircraft, which had entered service in April 1917, had sustained a rough baptism of

fire, four of six F.2A aircraft failing to return. But pilots soon realized what a machine they had in the Fighter, with the performance and agility of a single-seater combined with the sting in the tail of the two-seater. Once this lesson had been absorbed and the implications worked out, the Fighter became a formidable weapon.

The Germans were taken slightly unawares by the arrival of these latest Allied aircraft, and were slow to respond.

Firstly a new version of the Albatros appeared, the D V and D Va, with improved aerodynamics and a more powerful engine, but this machine proved entirely incapable of wresting from the Allies the superiority they enjoyed by the summer of 1917. Urgent requests for improved types were sent out, and in January 1918 the Fokker D VII was selected for quantity production. This was the war's best fighter.

In the field of bombing it was the

Russians, somewhat surprisingly, who led the way. The Russians realized that large aircraft would be needed to carry a significant quantity of bombs, and they already had such aircraft in the form of two four-engined machines, the *Russkii Vitiaz* and the *Le Grand*, both designed by Igor Sikorsky and built in 1913 by the Russian Baltic Railway Car Factory in St Petersburg as the world's first four-engined aircraft. Early in 1914 the Russian technical bureau ordered ten

OPPOSITE
The two-seat Airco D.H.4 day bomber, designed by Geoffrey de Havilland, marked the emergence of a new and highly capable type of warplane in the second half of World War I. The D.H.4 possessed the performance, especially in speed and ceiling, that gave it a considerable level of immunity from German fighter attack, and was also well armed. The type's only major limitation was the separation of the pilot and gunner by the main fuel tank in an arrangement that was dangerous and also limited tactical communication in the air.

RIGHT
The French counterpart of the D.H.4 was the Bréguet Bre.14 that could be operated in the bomber and escort fighter roles.

examples of an improved and enlarged version, the *Ilya Muromets*, as a bomber. Eventually some 80 of the type were built, but lack of suitable engines seriously hampered operational efforts. Nonetheless, over 400 sorties were flown with bomb loads of about 1,100lb (500kg). In reality, however, bombers of the size of the *Ilya Muromets* were inefficient even by the standards of the day.

Despite the efforts of the Royal Naval Air Service and the fledgling French bombing force, the Germans beat them to the first serious investigations of the possibilities of bombing. Here they had a head start, as a fair amount of preliminary work had been undertaken before the war during investigations into the use of Zeppelins as bombing craft. First into the field, during the summer of 1915, was the AEG G II, a large twin-engined biplane

bombers. These entered service in the first months of 1917 with both the Italian and French air services, and in Italian hands proved first-rate long-range aircraft. The British also decided to use heavy bombers, and their first effective type was the Handley Page O/100, which entered service in September 1916 and proved an immediate success, being capable of carrying some 2,000lb (907kg) of bombs. A more powerful version was designated O/400, and entered service in 1918.

Although heavy bombers pointed the way to the future, their military effect in World War I was minimal, and it was light bombers that played an important part in land operations during the closing stages of the war. Considering their importance, it is surprising that the Allies used only two basic types: the Airco (de Havilland) 4 and its two derivatives, the D.H.9 and 9a, and the French Bréguet Bre.14. The D.H.4 was in every respect one of the most remarkable aircraft of World War I. As well as being very agile and well armed it had a speed of 143mph (230km/h) when most fighters were only capable of

capable of delivering a 441-lb (200-kg) bomb load. This was joined in the autumn by the same company's G III, capable of lifting a 661-lb (300-kg) bomb load. A year later three other bombers had joined the German air service: the AEG G IV with an 882-lb (400-kg) bomb load, the Friedrichshafen G II with a 992-lb (450-kg) bomb load and the Gotha G III, also with a 992-lb (450-kg) bomb load. These aircraft served a useful purpose in paving the way for later types, but were not in themselves very successful. With the arrival of the Gotha G IV early in 1917, however, the Germans had at last found a useful long-range bomber. Zeppelins had been

launching sporadic attacks on targets in the southern half of the British Isles, principally London, since May 1915, but by 1917 the British defences had been so strengthened that Zeppelin losses were no longer tolerable. The Germans therefore decided to use the Gotha G IV and V over England, and the first Gotha raids were launched in June 1917 to the total consternation of public and government alike. Although the Zeppelin raids were the first strategic bombing ever attempted and had caused a great public shock, the aircraft raids proved a greater threat to life and property. There was an immediate outcry for the government to do

something to curb the German daylight raids. The raids continued into 1918, causing a steady stream of casualties and damage, despite the bolstering of the defence by squadrons removed from France. In 1918 the Gotha bombers were joined by a few Zeppelin (Staaken) R VI bombers, huge machines that could carry 4,409lb (2000kg) of bombs over short ranges.

The only other member of the Allied powers to have devoted some effort to strategic bombing early in the war was Italy, and early designs by Gianni Caproni proved excellent starting points for the Ca 3, 4 and 5 series of three-engined heavy

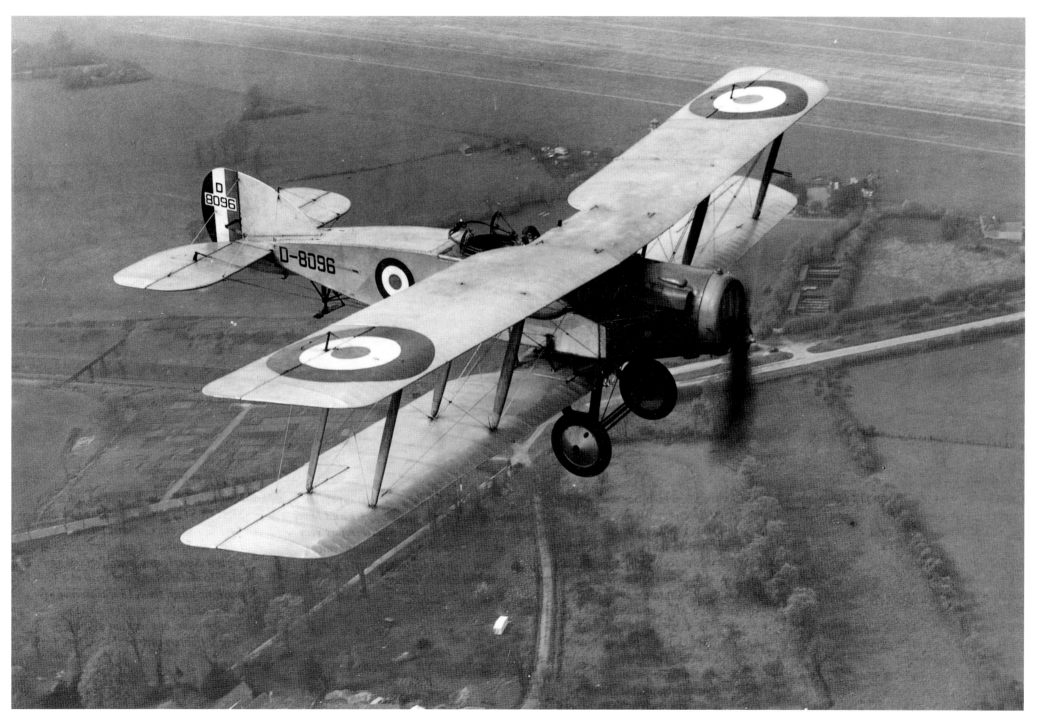

speeds in the region of 130mph (209km/h), and was capable of carrying a bomb load of 460lb (209kg). The D.H.4 entered service in 1917, and was joined in squadron use during 1918 by the supposedly improved D.H.9, which had the pilot's and observer's cockpits close together to obviate the D.H.4's main tactical failing, the near impossibility of the pilot and observer speaking to each other as they were separated by the bomb-bay. But reduced engine power meant that performance suffered badly, a factor only partially rectified by the development of the D.H.9a. The French

equivalent of these de Havilland bombers was the Bre.14, which began to enter service in September 1917. Sturdy and fairly fast, this bomber played an important part in harrying the retreating Germans in the second half of 1918, and also proved a more than adequate reconnaissance aircraft.

While the Allies concentrated on light bombers, the Germans placed more faith in ground-attack machines to support their land forces. These types were at first modified reconnaissance aircraft pending the arrival of more suitable, heavier, armoured designs such as the all-metal

ABOVE
The fuselage of the F.2B was supported by short struts between the upper and lower wings of the two-bay and therefore very strong wing cellule. The arrangement helped to provide the pilot with good forward fields of vision.

OPPOSITE
Seen with his French-supplied fighter, a SPAD S.XIII of the 94th Hat in the Ring Aero Squadron, Captain Edward V. Eddie Rickenbacker was the highest-scoring American ace of World War I with 26 victories. Armed with two Vickers machine-guns, the S.13 was immensely strong and also possessed high performance, but was not as agile as British fighters such as the Sopwith Camel.

OPPOSITE
The Pomilio PD was one of a series of two-seat warplanes that the Italians operated in the armed reconnaissance role, this example being armed with a 0.303-in (7.7-mm) Lewis fixed forward-firing machine-gun over the upper wing and a 0.256-in (6.5-mm) Revelli trainable rearward-firing machine-gun.

RIGHT
The Italians were among the first exponents of heavy bombing for strategic purposes, their Caproni company producing a number of types including the Ca 5 series that was built in a number of forms including, as its most numerous exemplar, the Ca 46 seen here. With its tail unit carried by two booms, the Ca 46 was powered by three Fiat engines as one driving a centreline pusher propeller and the other two powering tractor propellers at the front of the booms.

Junkers J 1, designed by Dr Hugo Junkers, one of the pioneers of metal construction. In the autumn of 1917, however, the need for a lighter type which could fulfil both the ground attack and reconnaissance roles became evident. The first of the new models, the Halberstadt CL II and Hannover CL II and III, were ready for the new squadrons to use with considerable success in the last-gasp German offensives in the spring and early summer of 1918. But useful as these new machines were in anticipating one of the major uses of armoured aircraft in World War II, the novel tactics and aircraft deployed by the Germans in 1918 were unable to overcome the clear supremacy of the Allies.

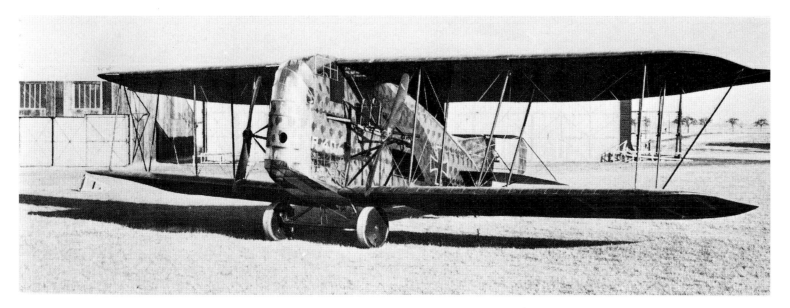

LEFT
Appearing in small numbers during 1918, the Farman F.50 was a two-seat night bomber able to carry eight 165-lb (75-kg) bombs, armed with one or two defensive machine-guns, and able to fly four hours on its powerplant of two 265-hp (198-kW) Lorraine-Dietrich engines.

BELOW LEFT
Germany placed considerable emphasis on the development of giant bombers, often with their engines located in the fuselage to drive wing-mounted propellers by means of long transmission shafts and angle-changing gearboxes. Few of these were successful, largely as a result of the unreliability of their transmission systems, and typical of the breed was the Link-Hofmann R I with a narrow but very deep fuselage completely filling the interplane gap.

OPPOSITE
The best heavy bomber to appear in World War I was a British machine, the Handley Page V/1500, but only three of these four-engined aircraft had been delivered before the end of the war.

Chapter Six

The Era of Racing and Record-Breaking Flight

If World War I had made aviation, the peace that followed almost broke the new industry. For the terrible cost of the war, both emotional and financial, put aviation back where it started in the last few years before 1914, at least from the constructors' and pilots' point of view. In those halcyon days there had been only a few hundred aircraft in the world (of perhaps 150 different types), with about three times that number of pilots. The war had brought vast and rapid growth: by the time of the Armistice in November 1918, France had built 68,000 aircraft, the UK 55,000, Germany 47,600, Italy 20,000, the USA 15,000 and Austria-Hungary 5,400. With the war ended by the Armistice that signalled the Allies' victory in November 1918, it was time to take stock of the consequences. Europe and the USA were dazed by the horrors of the war and the enormity of their losses; the people were all too ready to believe that World War I (or the Great War as it was then) had been the war to end all wars. After years of slaughter it was a natural reaction to turn away from all military machinery, including aviation; and the war's financial cost had an equally devastating impact on the industry. Europe was almost bankrupt. France, the UK and Italy had spent all, or almost all,

of their resources on the war and had then gone deep into debt with the USA to pay for the period 1917–18; Germany and Austro-Hungary were exhausted. There was no money in Europe for anything but essentials, and military spending was clearly not essential after the end of the war to end all wars. With the rundown of the world's major air forces, there was no work for the aircraft industries that supplied them.

More significant for aviation in general was the fact that a new generation

LEFT
Another British bomber that appeared too late for service in World War I was the twin-engined Vickers Vimy. This was a highly capable type powered by two powerful but reliable Rolls-Royce Eagle engines, and it was with a modified Vimy that Alcock and Brown made the first non-stop air crossing of the North Atlantic in 1919.

LEFT
Another British bomber that appeared too late for service in World War I was the twin-engined Vickers Vimy. This was a highly capable type powered by two powerful but reliable Rolls-Royce Eagle engines, and it was with a modified Vimy that Alcock and Brown made the first non-stop air crossing of the North Atlantic in 1919.

OPPOSITE
Only three examples of the three-seat Vimy bomber had been delivered before the Armistice that ended World War I in November 1918, but the type became standard in the Royal Air Force into the middle of the 1920s.

of aircraft was just entering service at the time of the Armistice, and it was immediately decided that these would be sufficient for peacetime. Thus the equipment of the Royal Air Force in the first years after the war consisted of the F.2B Fighter, Snipe, D.H.9a and Vimy machines. The first new bomber, the Fairey Fawn, did not enter service until 1923, and the first new fighters, in the forms of the Gloster Grebe and Armstrong Whitworth Siskin, came a year later. Although severe, the British government's cuts were matched

throughout most of Europe as well as in the USA.

Many aircraft manufacturers went out of business, in the process laying off many thousands of workers. Those left were faced with deciding what type of aircraft they should build. With no military demand, the only possibility was civil aviation. But what sort of aeroplane would sell? With money in short supply, the new aircraft would have to be not only cheap to buy and to run, but also cheap to produce, for none of the companies could afford much

experimental and development work. They had only one real hope: the civilian lightplane, meant for what was confidently expected to turn into a mass market within the next few years.

Early in the field were machines such as the Blackburn Sidecar and the Avro Baby, but with masses of wartime aircraft still on the market at very low prices their success was limited. Toward the middle of the 1920s, however, the British government decided to encourage these developments by sponsoring both lightplane competitions (and therefore

designs) and flying clubs, where the public might keep any machines they decided to buy. The first light aeroplane competition was organized by the Royal Aero Club, for which the Air Ministry provided some £3,000 in prizes. Among the entries were the Hawker Cygnet (the first design for the company by Sydney Camm, one of the greatest designers ever), the Shackleton ANEC, the English Electric Wren and the de Havilland D.H.53. The competition was a success but the public, wanting high performance and a good level of manoeuvrability,

expected too much of the lightplanes. One man who realized the implications of the lightplane's initial failure was Geoffrey de Havilland, the designer of the Moth. This beautiful little single-bay biplane combined reasonable performance and manoeuvrability with a fair amount of economy; powered by a 60-hp (44.7-kW) de Havilland Cirrus engine, it carried two people in tandem. The D.H.60 Moth was an immediate success and became the standard aeroplane found in the flying

clubs springing up first all over the UK, and then in the more advanced parts of the British Empire. Directly descended from the Moth itself came a line of aircraft culminating in the D.H.82 Tiger Moth, one of the most famous and best loved machines ever built. The success of the first Moth, moreover, persuaded other aircraft designers that this was the type of machine wanted by most would-be buyers; among several to follow in the Moth's footsteps were the Avro Avian,

the Westland Widgeon and the Avro Bluebird.

The USA, by contrast, showed little or no inclination toward private flying during the 1920s and no light aircraft worthy of note were produced. Commercial flying consisted mainly of aerial circuses, in which both men and women took part. The war had shown the public what aircraft could do, and the latter-day barnstormers were called upon to undertake the most hazardous of aerial

Economical and reliable one- and two-seat lightplanes were among the grails for which aircraft manufacturing companies sought in the 1920s in an effort to create and then satisfy a market that could provide an alternative to military aircraft as a source of work. This is an Avro Avian of the type used by celebrated pilots such as Bert Hinkler.

The Vickers Vimy of Alcock and Brown lifts off from an airstrip in Newfoundland during June 1919 at the start of the first successful non-stop flight across the North Atlantic.

the public's attention in the first years after the war.

In 1914 the *Daily Mail*, a great sponsor of aviation, had offered a prize of £10,000 for the first non-stop flight over the Atlantic. Several aircraft were being prepared or built for the event in the summer of 1914, but perhaps fortunately for their crews the outbreak of World War I put an end to these almost hopeless efforts. By 1919, however, aviation had advanced so far that a trans-Atlantic flight was a distinct possibility. The first successful crossing of the Atlantic was completed on 31 May 1919. Three Curtiss NC flying boats of the US Navy had set off from Rockaway, New York and, after stopping several times before reaching Newfoundland, had then set off for the Azores. Two came down before their objective, one sinking after its crew had been rescued, the other taxiing the last 200 miles (320km) across the water. From the Azores the remaining flying boat flew to Lisbon and finally to Ferrol in Spain, where it arrived after travelling almost 4,000 miles (6440km). This considerable achievement by the pilot, Commander A.C. Read, was proof that the Atlantic could be beaten. Of even greater importance, however, was the first non-stop crossing of the Atlantic. In a modified Vickers Vimy twin-engined bomber, Captain John Alcock and Lieutenant Arthur Whitten Brown set off from St Johns, Newfoundland, on 14 June 1919. Just under 16 hours later, on the 16th, they crash-landed in a bog near Clifden in County Galway, Ireland, after a flight of some 1,890 miles (3050km).

The 15 years following the end of World War I saw enormous advances in the theory and practice of flight. Speed,

exploits, including aerobatics, wing-walking, stepping from one aircraft in flight to another, and parachuting. Needless to say, accidents were frequent, but public demand had to be met if the circuses were to stay in business. The men who operated and flew in the circuses were normally ex-service pilots who could not settle down to a humdrum existence after the war. As the number of these pilots declined in the late 1920s and early 1930s and as the

growth of civil aviation began to attract governmental supervision and regulation, the flying circuses gradually died out.

Competitive aviation provided another outlet for the flying bug among wartime pilots, and this made a more dramatic appeal to the public. There were two types of competition: racing against other pilots over a particular course, and flying to establish records, particularly for absolute speed, altitude and distance. It was the latter that caught

range and altitude increased at an astonishing rate, and a host of other factors were improved. These factors were reflected most strongly in the aircraft that were created for record-breaking attempts and also for the speed-racing events that came to characterize the world of aviation during the 1920s.

Before World War I, pilots had on the whole been considered eccentric but interesting adventurers; the war itself had led to the cult of personality exemplified by the ace system for fighter pilots; now the public demanded the excitement and spectacle of daring men pushing themselves and their machines to their limits. In this respect, long-distance flights, such as those of Alcock and Brown and the other great pioneers, were matched only by the speed contests that tested the ultimate performance of men, aircraft and engines. Most countries with any significant interest in aviation held their own races, but it was in the USA that national racing really caught on in the years after the war.

The Pulitzer Trophy race was first held in 1920: it was a pure speed contest that would bring US Army and US Navy pilots and machines into intense rivalry. Although the series lasted only until 1925, it saw such legendary machines as the Verville-Sperry racer that won in

The Handley Page O/400 twin-engined heavy bomber, the most successful warplane of its type in World War I, provided the basis for a number of conversions as first-generation airliners after the end of the war, and helped to establish the manufacturer's credentials as a significant force in civil and transport aviation during the 1920s.

1920, and a series of great Curtiss racers. The other major competitions were the National Air Races, of which the two most important were the Thompson Trophy for speed round a closed-circuit course, and the Bendix Trophy for speed in a transcontinental race. US Army and US Navy aircraft entered these and other races, but they are remembered mostly for odd machines like the Gee Bee sportsters built by the Granville brothers, the Travel Air Mystery Ship and other out-and-out racers of dubious airworthiness but great power.

The blue riband of international competitive racing, however, was the contest for the Schneider Trophy. Now the permanent possession of the Royal Aero Club, this magnificent trophy was the prize in a series of races for aircraft that could operate from water. The series was instituted on 5 December 1912 by Jacques Schneider, the son of a leading French armaments manufacturer. Schneider had a vision of the world united by great flying boats, thus dispensing with the need for complex and costly airfields in remote corners of the earth. Henri Fabre of France had made the first flight from water only 30 months previously, on 28 March 1910, but Schneider's vision was by no means unique. He confidently expected that competition for his trophy would spur on developments in maritime aviation.

The contest for the trophy, which was to be held annually over a course of not less than 150 nautical miles (172.75 miles; 278km), was organized by the winner of the previous race. There were to be flotation and water navigation tests, and the series was to end when one team had won the contest three times in five years. Two contests were run before World War

I: the 1913 race, flown off Monaco, was won by Maurice Prévost of France in a Deperdussin, while the 1914 race, also held off Monaco, was won by Howard Pixton of the UK in a Sopwith Tabloid. The outbreak of World War 1 then prevented any British plans to stage the 1915 race.

By the time the series resumed in 1919, developments in aviation had completely changed the nature of the races, and also their place in history. The 1913 and 1914 winners had both been fast landplanes fitted with ill-designed floats, but in 1919 technical advances made during the war years were being incorporated into a new generation of flying boats. Aerodynamic advances had led to cleaner designs, producing less profile drag and less induced drag; engines had become more powerful and more reliable; improvements in the theory of structures and stressing enabled designers to build stronger and more refined airframes; and wartime pilots had made great advances in flying fast aircraft. By the same token it was no longer possible for a lone individual to enter the races with any real hope of winning. Manufacturers now sponsored their own machines, and as the pace of technological progress speeded up in the 1920s even major manufacturers found it impossible to finance entries. With this, the entry of government finance and technical backing by the armed forces was inevitable. By the end of the series its whole character had altered radically from that envisaged by Schneider. The aircraft that contested the final races were no longer flying boats, but special racing floatplanes, more advanced than their land-based contemporaries, constantly pushing on to and through the frontiers of knowledge.

Structures were pushed beyond their natural limits; new aerodynamics were investigated and incorporated; new fuels were developed; engines were constantly improved, their power/weight ratio in particular being advanced extremely rapidly; cooling systems moved into a new generation; and the skills of high-speed piloting were enhanced beyond all recognition. These advances came so soon, and were pushed on so fast, that when the UK won the Schneider Trophy outright in 1931, it took another four or five years for the rest of aeronautical development to catch up with the special floatplane racers. In effect, the work done on these machines laid the foundations for the technology that developed into the aircraft of World War II.

The 1919 race was declared void, the 1920 and 1921 races were both won by Italy, the 1922 race by the UK, the 1923 and 1925 races by the USA, the 1926 race by Italy, and the 1927 and 1929 races by the UK with the Supermarine S.5 and S.6 respectively. Assured by the prime minister, Ramsay MacDonald, that financial help would be available, the British now looked forward to the 1931 race and final victory. Yet, only 23 days after the UK's victory on 13 September, the government withdrew its support. Neither the money nor the RAF would be available; private enterprise would have to find its own resources. Rolls-Royce and Supermarine, the latter now part of the Vickers industrial empire, both wished to continue. After some effort they managed to persuade the government that it should pay for the further development of the R engine, and loan Vickers the two RAF-owned S.6 aircraft. Other conditions were impossible to meet, however, and the government refused to yield. Public

controversy reached a high peak and both parliament and the newspapers debated the matter over the next months. The government still would not budge, until in January 1931 Lady Houston, the widow of a shipping magnate, promised to foot the bill for the British effort. This, combined with public and press opinion, forced the government's hand and at the end of January 1931 the decision was made to allow the RAF to provide the men and technical expertise if Lady Houston and a few other backers would contribute the finance. Little time was left, so Reginald Mitchell decided that the only solution was to modify the S.6 into an S.6B accommodating the improved and more powerful engine; other changes were a longer fuselage and larger floats.

The Italians had returned to the drawing-board for their 1931 design, which again teamed the firms of Macchi and Fiat. The result of this partnership was the Macchi-Castoldi MC.72, powered by the remarkable AS6 engine driving contra-rotating propellers in an effort to overcome the torque problems that bedevilled seaplane racing craft as power outputs rose towards and past 1,000hp (746kW). Development of this promising idea took longer than expected, however, and after a fatal crash the Italian team was withdrawn from the 1931 race. Once again, the French wished to enter, but were unable to raise a team. Consequently, the UK had only to get an aircraft round the course to win the Schneider Trophy outright. On 13 September 1931, in a sad anti-climax to a protracted struggle, Flight-Lieutenant J.N. Boothman flew his S.6B round the Calshot course at 340.08mph (547km/h) to win the trophy for the UK. The Schneider Trophy races were at last over.

The last two racers, the S.6B and the MC.72, went on to set up new world air speed records: on 29 September 1931 the S.6B reached 407.5mph (656km/h), and on 23 October 1934 the MC.72 reached 440.7mph (709.2km/h).

The Schneider Trophy races, the blue riband of air racing, made several material contributions to the advancement of aviation. Rather than aerodynamics, aero engine development was the main benefactor, together with fuels and to some extent propellers. Nonetheless, it was on these aircraft that the great designers of Italy and the UK came to grips with advanced aerodynamics, and this applies particularly to Reginald Mitchell and Mario Castoldi, two of the most significant designers of the middle and late 1930s. Quite apart from the technical benefits, moreover, the Schneider Trophy races helped to keep aviation in the public eye at a time when there was little money for aviation in general, and passenger flying was only for the few.

Racing series like the Schneider Trophy competitions produced the ultimate aircraft of the period, when measured in terms of performance at any cost. Yet the same period in the late 1920s and early 1930s saw another type of competitive flying: record-breaking flights over increasingly long distances. While the purely speed contests required advanced technology and received government sponsorship, long-distance flying was generally the domain of private pilots.

The technical requirements for speed racing and for distance flying were, inevitably, completely different. Where the speed racers could exploit technical advances to the maximum, in airframes, engines and fuels, aircraft designed for long-distance flying placed far greater emphasis on reliability. Thus they generally pushed forward the boundaries of existing technology rather than broke aerodynamic and metallurgical boundaries.

The engines of speed racers, for example, needed to deliver very high power for only a few hours before wearing out; the engines of long-distance aircraft, on the other hand, were required to run for a long period at a steady if unspectacular output. Failure to do so could easily force the distance flyer down into the vastness of some ocean or desert, or indeed in any of the world's other inhospitable regions. Furthermore, long-distance aircraft had to provide at least a modicum of comfort to mitigate the onset of pilot fatigue, and for the same reason needed basically sound flying characteristics. In practical terms, the most immediate beneficiaries of such long-distance flying were the burgeoning number of civil airlines, especially those that were starting to provide regular services. Bombers also derived benefits

from the experience of long-distance flying and aircraft: as a direct result, navigational skills increased and machines capable of carrying a significant payload began to appear on the designers' drawing boards.

There had been a number of pioneering long-distance flights immediately after World War I, the most notable being the first crossing of the Atlantic by American Curtiss seaplanes, and the first non-stop Atlantic crossing by Alcock and Brown, both in 1919. The aircraft used in these flights were basically World War I types modified for the specific demands of these epoch-making flights, but from the early 1920s long-distance flights were made in an increasing number of new aircraft. In 1924, four Douglas World Cruisers of the US Army departed on the first flight round the world. Departing from Seattle, Washington, on 6 April, the four aircraft flew via the Aleutian Islands, Japan and India, through Europe to Scotland, Iceland and Greenland, and so back to Seattle. Two of the aircraft arrived back at their departure point on 28 September after a remarkable journey which had lasted 175 days. Although the average speed of the aircraft was slow, the achievement was an extraordinary one in every other respect. The mere fact that two of the four aircraft, operating from wheeled or float landing gear as required, had even managed to fly around the world was in itself a great feat, especially considering the inhospitality of some of the areas through which they passed. The next round-the-world flight was not made until five years later, when the *Graf Zeppelin*, an airship, achieved the feat in 21 days, 7 hours and 34 minutes. It was a further two years before another heavier-

OPPOSITE
Though not characterized by high speed or individually long stages, the flight round the world by the Douglas World Cruiser of the US Army was an extraordinary feat of technical endurance proving the reliability of the airframe and the engine.

ABOVE
The Bréguet Bre.19 sesquiplane was produced in a number of operational and record-breaking forms, the latter with increasingly large fuel capacities for very-long-range flights.

than-air craft flew round the world again.

There followed a number of other attempts on the Atlantic, both successful and unsuccessful, before the greatest of all the early long-distance flights. On 20/21 May 1927 Captain Charles A. Lindbergh flew across the North Atlantic from Long Island, New York, to Paris. The world was astounded by the achievement and heroism of this unknown American pilot flying a specially built aeroplane, the Ryan NYP named *Spirit of St Louis*. Lindbergh's flight was a landmark in every respect. It was the first solo non-stop transatlantic flight and, unlike earlier pioneers, Lindbergh had flown in effect from one major city to another. Alcock and Brown, for example, had set off from Newfoundland, the most easterly point in

the Americas, and landed near Clifden in County Galway, on Ireland's western coast, thus making their crossing by the shortest possible route. Lindbergh had taken off just outside New York and landed just outside Paris, so winning the $25,000 prize offered by Raymond Orteig for the first New York-Paris or Paris-New York flight.

Lindbergh's place in aviation history rests on the remarkable achievement of his flight between New York and Paris, the preparations for which were almost entirely his own work. His success also served to stimulate other aviators keen to make their mark on history. Shortly after Lindbergh's flight, Clarence Chamberlin, with C.A. Levine as his passenger, attempted a non-stop flight from just

outside New York to Berlin. Chamberlin took off in his Wright-Bellanca W.B.2 monoplane, *Columbia*, on 4 June 1927, but came down in Eisleben, well short of Berlin, two days later after a flight of 3,911 miles (6294km). Flights across the Atlantic still beckoned the adventurous, but there now followed a series of disastrous failures. F.F. Minchin, L. Hamilton and the Princess Loewenstein-Wertheim were lost over the North Atlantic during an attempt to fly from the UK to Canada; and the great British pioneer airline pilot, Captain W.G.R. (Bert) Hinchcliffe, together with the Hon. Elsie Mackay, also died in the ocean.

Finally, a successful east-to-west crossing was made. Captain Hermann Köhl, Colonel James Fitzmaurice and Günther, Graf von Hünefeld left Baldonnel, Ireland, in a Junkers F 13 named *Bremen*, and landed on Greenly Island off Labrador one day later on 13 April 1928. The Atlantic had now been conquered in both directions and the great feats of long-distance flying moved elsewhere. Even so, the Atlantic still exerted a strong pull on would-be record breakers, and many who would win fame for other flights served their apprenticeship crossing the North and South Atlantic. The high-wing Fokker monoplanes were now at their peak: in 1928 Amelia Earhart, an American pilot destined for a mysterious end, crossed from west to east as a passenger in a Fokker, while Charles Kingsford-Smith made an east-west crossing, also in a Fokker.

Pilots were now attempting increasingly lengthy routes: for example, on 15/16 July 1931 the Hungarians Gyorgy Endres and Alexander Magyar flew from Newfoundland to Budapest in

their Lockheed Model 8 *Sirius*, and on 28/30 July 1931 Russell Boardman and John Polando flew a Bellanca from New York to Istanbul. By 10 August 1934 the North Atlantic had been flown 45 times, in all cases but four by heavier-than-air machines. By the end of September 1934 the South Atlantic had also been flown many times: 31 crossings, all by heavier-than-air craft.

Other long-distance flights, often as difficult but generally less well known, were also being tried. In 1920, for example, a small fleet of Italian aircraft comprising four Caproni and seven SVA aircraft set off from Rome to fly to Tokyo in a journey that was more fraught with difficulties than can easily be imagined. The aircraft had to cross some of the most desolate and backward areas in the world. Of the 11 aircraft only two SVA machines reached Tokyo, one flown by Masiero and the other by Ferrarin, who later made a great name for himself both in the Schneider Trophy races and with several record-breaking flights over long distance. It had taken the two Italians almost three months to make the trip.

Other great flights to the Far East were those of Pelletier d'Oisy and Bésin, who took a little less than seven weeks to fly a Bréguet Bre.19GR from Paris to Tokyo in 1924, and de Pinedo and Campanelli who in 1925 flew from Lake Maggiore to Tokyo and back in a Savoia-Marchetti flying boat. The outward leg of this 34,000-mile (54720-km) journey included a flight round Australia. In the same year, Pelletier d'Oisy flew from Paris to Peking in the remarkably short time of one week. The most famous Bre.19 was the one named *Point d'Intérrogation* (question mark), flown from Paris to New York by Costes and Bellonte of France on

1/2 September 1930. Unusually for the period, the Bre.19 was a military aeroplane, specially adapted with extra fuel tankage, at a time when most other long-distance machines were built specifically for this task or alternatively adapted from civil machines that had already proved their range capabilities.

After the conquest of the North and South Atlantic the great challenge of long-distance flight was the mighty Pacific Ocean. The first crossing had been made during the US Army's round-the-world flight in 1924, when the four Douglas World Cruisers had flown from the Aleutian Islands to Japan. A gap of almost three years followed before the next attempt: on 1 June 1927, Lieutenants Lester Maitland and Albert Hegenberger flew a Fokker C-2 *Bird of Paradise* transport over the 2,400 miles (3860km) from Oakland, California to Honolulu in the Hawaiian Islands in a fraction under 26 hours.

So great are the distances involved

that it was quite out of the question for aircraft of the 1920s and early 1930s to fly non-stop across the full breadth of the Pacific Ocean. The main routes between land masses therefore became the important factors. The first man to make the significant crossing from the USA to Australia was Squadron-Leader Charles Kingsford-Smith, with fellow Australian Flight-Lieutenant Charles Ulm and Americans Harry Lyons and J.W. Warner as crew. In the now famous Fokker F VII/3m *Southern Cross*, Kingsford-Smith and his crew set off from Oakland on 31 May 1928. Flying via Honolulu and Fiji, a remarkable feat of navigation, Kingsford-Smith and his crew arrived in Brisbane, Queensland on 10 June after a nine-day flight. The Fokker type of high-wing monoplane had particularly good range, and was doing well in both civil and military service. Flying a Lockheed Model 8 Altair, Kingsford-Smith, now knighted and with Captain Taylor as his crew, made the first crossing of the Pacific in a single-engined aeroplane between 22 October and 4 November 1934. His route was the reverse of the one he had taken in 1928. This great flight provides striking evidence that confidence in the reliability of aircraft and their engines had increased still further.

Women played their own part in the conquest of the Pacific: on 11/12 January 1935 Amelia Earhart became the first woman to fly across the ocean when she took a Lockheed Model 5 Vega from Oakland to Honolulu. On 20/21 May 1932, as Mrs Putnam, she had also made the first solo west-to-east crossing of the North Atlantic by a woman, flying from Harbour Grace, Newfoundland, to Londonderry in Northern Ireland. One of the greatest women pilots ever, Amelia

Earhart was finally lost on the trans-Pacific leg of an attempted round-the-world flight in 1937.

While pilots of all nations, together with American civilian aviators, were concentrating their efforts on record-breaking flights across the major oceans, pilots of the US Army made a number of remarkable flights within their own large country. In September 1922, for example, Lieutenant James Doolittle, later a celebrated Schneider Trophy pilot and leader of the famous Doolittle Raid on Tokyo in 1942, made a great flight across the USA from Jacksonville, Florida to San Diego, California. He completed the journey in just over 21 hours, with only one refuelling stop, in an Airco D.H.4 built in the USA as a de Havilland DH-4 Liberty Plane. Eight months later,

Lieutenants John Macready and Oakley Kelly flew a single-engined Fokker T-2 over a non-stop distance of 2,500 miles (4025km) from New York in just under 27 hours. The two men had only just established a world duration record of just over 36 hours in the same machine. June 1924 saw yet another triumph for the US Army when Lieutenant Russell Maughan raced the sun across the USA in a Curtiss PW-8 fighter from New York to San Francisco, a distance of 2,670 miles (4300km). A further advance in long-distance flying was made during the first week of January 1929, when a Fokker C-2A was kept in the air for 150 hours with the aid of air-to-air refuelling. The aeroplane, named *Question Mark*, was crewed by Major Carl Spaatz, Captain Ira Eaker, Lieutenants Harry Halverson and

Elwood Quesada, and Sergeant Roy Hoe: all four officers were to rise to high command in World War II. In the course of the flight the C-2A was refuelled no less than 37 times from a Douglas O-2C, which also supplied oil and other necessary items. The technique was rudimentary, to say the least, requiring someone in the C-2A to grasp the hose as it was lowered from the O-2C and then lower the nozzle into the opened filler of the fuel tank before reversing the process at the end of the refuelling. Nevertheless the experiment was successful and paved the way for the air-to-air refuelling techniques now vital for any modern air force.

The private individuals who had dominated the sport so far were setting their sights on greater objectives. Perhaps the most adventurous of these men were

N965Y

OPPOSITE
Coming to rival Lindbergh as a world-wide celebrity in the early 1930s was perhaps the greatest of all female long-distance fliers, the American Amelia Earhart, seen here with the Lockheed Vega high-wing cantilever monoplane on which she recorded some of her best flights.

RIGHT
Used as a small-capacity commercial transport as well as for a host of great long-distance flights, the Lockheed Vega helped to establish its manufacturer as a major force and marked a transitional point in the evolution of the transport from a fabric-covered biplane of largely wooden construction to a cantilever monoplane with a stressed-skin structure that was of wood in the Vega but soon of metal in more advanced aircraft.

Wiley Post and Harold Gatty. Like Hinchliffe and Coli, who had both disappeared over the Atlantic, Post was blind in one eye, and habitually wore a black patch. Flying possibly the best long-range type of the period, a Lockheed Model 5 Vega named *Winnie Mae of Oklahoma*, Post and Gatty set off from New York early on 23 June 1931. Stopping to refuel at Harbour Grace in Newfoundland, Chester in England, Berlin, Moscow, Novosibirsk, Blagoveshchensk, Khabarovsk, Fairbanks in Alaska and Edmonton in Canada, Wiley and Post returned to New York on 1 July after an heroic flight of eight days.

The next round-the-world flight was made by Herndon and Pangborn in a Bellanca, and took 81 days. Then followed the first circumnavigation by a flying boat, a Dornier Wal flown by

Wolfgang von Gronau, Gerd von Roth, Fritz Albrecht and Franz Hack, in 111 days between 21 July and 9 November 1932.

The greatest long-distance flight of the period, however, took place when Wiley Post flew solo round the world in the remarkable time of 7 days, 18 hours and 49 minutes, between 15 and 22 July 1933, when he arrived back in New York to a tumultuous welcome.

Most of the famous long-distance flights, especially those made by

Americans and Italians, were undertaken in monoplanes. In the middle 1920s the USA and Italy had taken a distinct lead over the rest of the world in the development of such long-range monoplanes. The British, on the other hand, were concentrating on developing the last ounce of benefit from the tried and tested biplane formula which had proved so successful during World War I, for the legacy of the War Office's short and misjudged ban on monoplanes as being potentially dangerous was still with

the country. Some interesting monoplane designs had reached prototype form, but these had for the most part been either very large, such as the Rohrbach-Beardmore Inflexible bomber and the Fairey Long-Range Monoplane, or very small lightplanes such as the Blackburn Sidecar (dating from 1918), the Short-Gnosspelius Gull, and a variety of other Short machines. In both these categories, monoplane design was the only practical possibility, for biplane construction was too heavy and clumsy for large aircraft,

and produced too much drag for very small aircraft.

Yet no sooner had World War I ended than British aviators were off on a variety of flights to what were to prove their most successful stamping grounds: Africa, India and Australia.

The most important of the British pioneers of long-distance flight was Alan Cobham, the complete practical aviator

who also possessed the personality and dynamism to infect others with his ideas. Born in 1894, Cobham served in the Royal Flying Corps and then the RAF during World War I, and joined the new de Havilland company when this was created after the war to succeed Airco. Cobham was a true enthusiast of civil aviation, and his proving flights did much to pave the way for the development of

civil air routes. His personality and writings were equally influential, and were largely responsible for the development of civil air-mindedness in the UK. On 16 November 1925 Cobham set off in his D.H.50 to fly to Cape Town and back, a distance of some 16,000 miles (25750km) which he flew in four months. Knighted after this flight, Cobham now set his sights on the route

to Australia. Again in the D.H.50, Cobham took off with his mechanic from Rochester in Kent on 30 June 1926, arriving in Melbourne five weeks later, on 5 August. The next month Cobham left for England again, arriving in London on 1 October after a flight of 27 days. The significance of Cobham's flights lay not in their speed, but in their consistency and planning, for Cobham was interested primarily in proving that the distance could be flown safely in a number of legs, and in validating the concept that if airfields with fuel and maintenance facilities were located at strategic intervals along the route, this would make it not just feasible but fully practical to inaugurate passenger transport to the farther reaches of the empire. During the same period, while he was making his great proving flights, Cobham also entered several air races, and started a campaign to persuade the British that each major town should have its own airfield. He toured Africa in a flying boat, the Short *Singapore*, during 1927 and 1928, and made other important flights before starting his National Aviation Day Campaign in 1932. This took the form of a travelling air display and very many Britons must have made their first flight in one of Cobham's aircraft when the display arrived at their home town.

The period also saw some remarkable flights by the Fairey Long-Range Monoplane on the Africa and India routes. On 24/26 April 1929 an RAF crew consisting of Squadron-Leader A.G. Jones-Williams and Flight-Lieutenant N.H. Jenkins flew the Fairey non-stop from Cranwell in Lincolnshire to Karachi, now Pakistan, in 50 hours 48 minutes, the first ever such flight. Then, on 6/8 February 1933, Squadron-Leader O.R. Gayford and Flight-Lieutenant G.E. Nicholetts flew from Cranwell to Walvis Bay in South-West Africa, a distance of 5,309 miles (8544km) in 57 hours 30 minutes.

So far these British distance flights had been conducted only against the clock or to prove that the flight could be made. In 1934, however, the classic MacPherson Robertson (generally abbreviated to MacRobertson) air race from London to Melbourne took place. This marked the beginning of a new age in aviation. The race attracted an odd assortment of aircraft, ranging from the sleek and beautiful de Havilland D.H.88 Comets, designed specially for the race, via a number of comparatively advanced airliners, to a de Havilland D.H.89 Dragon Rapide biplane air transport. The results of the race, in which a Comet won but was closely followed by a fully laden but unmodified Douglas DC-2 entered by the Dutch national airline, KLM, did a great deal to persuade European designers to turn their attention to the design features of the new breed of American airliner: all-metal construction, a low-mounted cantilever monoplane wing, and well-cowled radial engines.

Chapter Seven
Commercial Aviation –
A Hesitant Start

Racing series like the Schneider Trophy competitions produced the ultimate aircraft of the period, when measured in terms of performance at any cost. Yet the same period in the late 1920s and early 1930s saw another type of competitive flying: record-breaking commercial transport in heavier-than-air craft had started in the months immediately after the end of World War I, but initial success was no guarantee of long-term viability. Neither the machines nor the routes were satisfactory at first. The aircraft were World War I bombers adapted for the role of passenger-carrying. This meant that the interior of the wooden-framed and fabric-covered fuselage was converted to accommodate a limited number of passengers, while the rest of the airframe was left unaltered. Conditions for the passengers were spartan, for the cabin was both cold and draughty.

The routes, meanwhile, served short-term political interests rather than long-term economic ones. Linking the capitals of the victorious nations, principally France and the UK, they allowed diplomats, civil servants and politicians to untangle the complex political and financial legacy of the war with the greatest possible speed. These fledgling routes were open to the general public

LEFT
The Boeing company began to come to the fore after World War I, one of its first products being the Model C floatplane in which William E. Boeing (right) and his pilot, Eddie Hubbard, on 3 March 1919 flew the first international air mail service between Seattle, Washington, in the USA's north-western corner to Vancouver in the Canadian province of British Columbia.

OPPOSITE
A pair of very sensibly attired ladies prepare to board an extemporized transport aeroplane, converted from an Airco D.H.9 bomber by de Havilland, during the early 1920s.

but private passengers needed to be wealthy and interested as much in the novelty of air transport as in getting to their destinations quickly. A market of this type, depending on a small and short-lived passenger base, could not allow the evolution of a sound airline business.

Gradually the number and extent of airline routes began to grow, however, as airlines realized that joyriding passengers could, and in the long-term must, be supplemented by businessmen and other

travellers who had a vested financial reason for rapid transport.

As the airlines that had survived the first heady months of peace started to rationalize their routes in the early 1920s, the generation of converted wartime machines was being phased out in favour of newer types designed specifically for the air transport role. Age was beginning to catch up with the initial conversions, and the new breed of passenger was not prepared to put up with the discomfort of such machines. First progress was made in Germany, where there were several excellent and farsighted designers. By the terms of the Treaty of Versailles, Germany was not allowed to design, build or possess any military aircraft, so German designers was perforce limited to civil types. This concentration of effort greatly aided the production of the world's first proper airliner, discounting the Sikorsky *Le Grand* of 1913. This was the Junkers J 13, later redesignated F 13, which appeared in 1919 and entered service with Deutsche Luft Hansa shortly afterwards. (The airline's name was altered to Deutsche Lufthansa later in the 1920s.)

The J 13 bore a clear family relationship to the low-wing cantilever metal fighters and ground-attack aircraft that Junkers had produced toward the end of the war, and was so different in overall concept that it met with considerable resistance at first. The low wing position, it was claimed, would make the centre of gravity too high, and the metal structure was also considered suspect. But the J 13 was years ahead of its time, as later events were to prove: apart from the clumsiness of the engine installation and the standard fixed landing gear with a spreader bar, the J 13 had lines that were sleek by the standards of the day and carried its pilot and four

passengers in the relative comfort of an enclosed cockpit and cabin respectively. Hugo Junkers went on to produce other very successful airliners, most of them featuring the type of corrugated Dural skinning Junkers had taken up in the war when steel skinning proved too heavy.

By the standards of the early 1920s the Junkers airliners were very advanced. British and French transports of the period were clumsy and old-fashioned in appearance, having the biplane configuration with its attendant mass of rigging and bracing wires. The only other manufacturer to match the Junkers advances was Anthony Fokker, who had spent the war years in Germany where his company produced a number of important training and fighter designs for the Imperial German Air Service. An astute businessman, Fokker had realized in 1918 that Germany was about to lose the war, and prepared for flight accordingly. Dutch by birth, he had managed to cross over into the neutral Netherlands at the end of the war with a train carrying large numbers of dismantled aircraft, engines, tools, machines, and plans. Using money salted away in easier times, Fokker was able to set up in business again in his native country. He found a ready market for his World War I designs in the Netherlands and Sweden, and then set about developing new military and civil aircraft. Although his fighting machines were to achieve some success in the next few years, it was civil aircraft that really made Fokker's reputation in the 1920s and 1930s. As his chief designer he had the untrained, intuitive and retiring Reinhold Platz, one of the ablest designers to emerge from World War I, as shown by his great Dr I, D VII and D VIII fighters

LEFT
The Junkers G 38 four-engined airliner of all-metal construction was an extraordinary four-engined machine that was in effect a flying wing with a small fuselage to carry the tail unit required for longitudinal and directional control. There were windowed passenger compartments in the leading edges of the wings' inner sections adjacent to the fuselage.

OPPOSITE
Another all-metal type, with the same type of corrugated skinning as the Junkers aircraft of the period, was the Ford Tri-Motor, which was conceptually inspired by the Fokker F.VII-3m tri-motor.

of 1917 and 1918. Platz saw no reason to abandon the constructional features that had contributed so much to the success of the three fighters, and set about producing civil airliners with the same clean lines, simplicity and strength.

The first such airliner to enter service was the F II, which appeared in 1920. This was a typical Platz design: a welded steel-tube fuselage of rectangular section covered with canvas except for the engine cowling, which was covered with metal sheeting; sturdy but simple landing gear; and a massive cantilever wing covered with plywood. Platz favoured thick wings for two main reasons: they made possible the use of box spars (spars with a hollow rectangular cross-section) of great depth and strength, and also produced a fair amount of lift, for which Platz was prepared to pay the price in drag. As usual with his designs, Platz located the wing on top of the fuselage. This left the fuselage entirely clear for the passengers;

allowed the construction of a single-piece wing that was very strong; and also gave a measure of pendulum stability to the whole aeroplane.

The contrast in wing location between Junkers and Fokker aircraft provoked much discussion at the time. Platz could scarcely be faulted by the standards of the day, before retractable landing gear came into use. The F II paved the way for a series of steadily improving transports that reached their technical and commercial apogee with the F VII family comprising the original single-engined F VII, aerodynamically enhanced F VIIA, F VIIA/3m tri-motor and long-range F VIIB/3m tri-motor versions. The family constituted possibly the most successful airliners and long-distance record breakers of the period, and contributed beyond measure to the acceptance of long-distance flying as a normal part of airline operations.

The influence of Fokker airliners on other designers was nowhere more apparent than in the best American airliner of the 1920s, the Ford Tri-Motor. This appeared in June 1926 and combined what the designer, William Stout, thought to be the best features of both the Fokker and Junkers type of aircraft: the Tri-Motor resembled the Fokker F VIIA/3m in appearance, but was built with the Junkers type of corrugated skinning. Eloquent testimony to the ruggedness and basic strength of the Tri-Motor is provided by the fact that a few were still in service in South America 50 years after their introduction.

Junkers had not been standing idle all this time: the company had produced a series of typical Junkers aircraft, culminating in the G 31 of 1926. This was a tri-motor transport powered by

LEFT
The cabin of the Ford Tri-Motor reveals the considerably greater levels of roominess and comfort enjoyed by the passengers of the late 1920s and early 1930s, although their aircraft were also noisier and very much slower than modern airliners.

OPPOSITE
Built only in small numbers, the Handley Page H.P.42 series of four-engined biplane airliners could best be described as stately, for they were slow but also very reliable and offered high levels of comfort and service.

three 450-hp (335.5-kW) radial engines, and could carry 16 passengers at 100mph (160km/h). Like the F VII, it had a wide-track split landing gear, and in turn proved the starting point for further Junkers aircraft, which culminated in the single-engined Ju 52 of 1930 and its three-engined derivative, the Ju 52/3m which became the most famous and prolific German transport of the 1930s and World War II. Like the Tri-Motor, the Ju 52/3m remained in service for many years, and its ruggedness and wide-track landing gear proved invaluable for operations on and off mediocre if not poor airfields.

By the middle of the 1920s, most European nations had established their own national airlines. Companies such as Fokker sold its transports to the airlines of most technically advanced nations, but the general tendency was for the national flag-carrying airline to operate machines built in the same country. Imperial Airways, the British airline, operated a variety of types, the most important early machine being the de Havilland D.H.66 Hercules. This was typical of the design

Iraq, at the convergence of the Euphrates and Tigris rivers, and finally to Karachi then in north-western India during 1929. The British transport used most frequently on European routes was the Armstrong Whitworth Argosy, another cumbersome biplane of tri-motor and triple-finned design.

Imperial Airways ordered two versions of one basic biplane type for its European and intercontinental routes: these four-engined Handley Page aircraft were the H.P.45 Heracles carrying 38 passengers on European routes, and the H.P.42 Hannibal carrying 24 passengers over long distances. In their way these were great aircraft, for in their years of service not one passenger suffered an injury. Both variants had the triple fins and rudders that were almost the trademark of British airliners in this period.

France was also behind the times, and only acquired a national airline, Air France, in 1933. As in the UK, various airlines had concentrated their primary commercial efforts on services to the farther-flung parts of the French Empire. Unlike the British, however, the French had relatively few stepping stones to the Far East, and so placed great reliance on a series of old-fashioned Lioré-et-Olivier (LeO) and Bréguet flying boats, the best means of air travel to the remoter parts of the world as they required no airfields of the type that were and still are the single most expensive item in the infrastructure required to support airline operations. Italy, on the other hand, used the excellent tri-motor monoplanes (most of them produced by Caproni and Savoia) as well as a miscellany of smaller types for its airline routes within Europe and across the Mediterranean to Libya and thence to Italian Somaliland. In common with

practices used in British transport aircraft in the mid-1920s: it was a large machine with wide-track landing gear, a slab-sided fuselage mounted over the lower unit of the biplane wing cellule, and a tail unit carrying triple fins and rudders of classic de Havilland shape mounted above the monoplane tailplane and elevator. The spacious 14-passenger cabin was located over the lower wing, and the three engines were mounted in the nose of the fuselage and above the main landing gear wheels, one in each lower wing. With a cruising speed just under 100mph (160km/h), the Hercules was employed mainly on the intercontinental flights operated by Imperial Airways, first to Egypt, then in 1927 to Basra in southern countries such as Germany, Italy made great efforts to produce transport aircraft that were highly cost-effective as they could be used as airliners in times of peace, and as troop transports or even primitive bombers in times of war. Another attraction of this operational philosophy for the Germans and Italians, moreover, was the fact that the relevant production lines could quickly be adapted to produce a dedicated warplane modelled on the basic transport's combination of airframe and powerplant. This had obvious advantages in the rapid production of military aircraft, and also opened the possibility of reduced development and production costs, which was a factor of considerable importance to a country such as Italy, which was relatively underdeveloped so far as its industrial base was concerned. For Germany, the policy had a most sinister rationale as the country was prohibited by the Treaty of Versailles from developing and/or producing any military aircraft: dual-role aircraft could thus be passed off as civil transports rather than bombers.

This aspect of German aircraft development and production was not particularly significant in the late 1920s and early 1930s, but it became of paramount importance between the time that the Nazis had come to power in 1933 and Hitler's rejection of the treaty structures in 1935.

Even if its aircraft did not have an overt military aspect, Lufthansa had considerably greater numbers of flying personnel than other airlines in relation to the number of aircraft it operated. This was because the Germans had discovered early in the 1920s that by training an excess of pilots and navigators they could produce the aircrew that would be

essential to the effective rearmament of Germany once this was set in hand. Supported by the clandestine air ministry, Lufthansa kept a large number of training aircraft on which those aircrew not engaged on active airline operations could develop their skills.

On the other side of the Atlantic, the American airline industry was almost non-existent during the 1920s. The main regions of population were linked by an extremely efficient network of roads and railways, and mass-production was already making the car part of every home. Long

air flights involved noise, a considerable amount of dirt and refuelling stops every couple of hundred miles: by comparison, trains and buses provided a higher level of comfort, little noise, fewer refuelling stops and lower cost. With the exception of those to Canada, Mexico and the closer islands in the Caribbean, there were no external routes for the Americans to launch, for the distances involved in intercontinental routes were far beyond the technology of the time. The only possible routes with an economic future were those to the main cities of Canada,

A giant of its time, the 12-engined Dornier Do X flying boat was not a success at the technical level and therefore never placed in service, but presaged the level of comfort and amenity that would soon be provided to passengers travelling long-range routes on flying boat airliners created by Boeing, Martin, Short and Sikorsky.

The economics of the fledgling American airline industry in the late 1920s and early 1930s meant that air mail had to be carried, with surplus volume available for the movement of passengers. Seen in 1930, this Boeing Model 40A could carry four passengers as well as mail on Boeing Air Transport's route linking San Francisco, California and Chicago, Illinois.

Then, in one of those extraordinary reversals that seem to characterize the period, the government took over all these private-enterprise airfields, and in return put the mail flights themselves out to commercial tender. The change was ultimately to the benefit of US commercial aviation since the government was in a position to improve airfields and navigational aids such as radio; it also ensured adequate maintenance for all the mailplanes. The mail had to be delivered in all weathers to meet the terms of the contract, which paid by the ton of mail collected and delivered, and this had a great effect in spurring the development of fast all-weather aircraft capable of carrying a reasonable payload.

The development of such aircraft, even in the limited numbers required or the servicing of the nation's airmail network, laid the foundations on which American civil aviation began to grow into the towering giant it is today: the manufacturers produced the required technological developments; the routes opened up the best courses between the main cities; nocturnal and, more importantly, all-weather flying improved piloting and navigational skills, and also proved the need for blind-flying instruments; and the whole operation showed the American people some of the benefits that could result from fast and reliable air services.

In 1927 Boeing, soon to emerge as a giant of the aeronautical world, made an extremely low tender for the Chicago to San Francisco route, and to the amazement of the pundits actually made a profit on the contract. The plane used was the Boeing Model 40A, for its time a remarkably efficient and economical aeroplane, though not at all radical in its

but these were mostly close to the border and already well linked with the USA by road and rail.

There were several small private operators, however, and these operated limited services in heavily populated areas and places where road and rail transport was difficult, as well as services to the holiday centres of the Caribbean. Moreover, the Americans did develop a remarkable and forward-looking route network for the carriage of mail. Organized by the US Post Office, the airmail service started in May 1918 with a service between New York and Washington, DC, but was soon expanded right across the continent to San Francisco in California. The inauguration and subsequent development of the network was beset by a number of technical and operational problems, but by 1925 a crude yet increasingly serviceable navigation system was available across the centre of the continent: this consisted of great blazes about 25 miles (40km) along each route, with all the airfields revealed and illuminated by searchlights.

OPPOSITE
Steady improvements in aerodynamics and structures combined with the development of the air-cooled radial engine to allow the design and manufacture of fast, reliable and economic light transport aircraft such as the Travel Air 5000, seen here with the celebrated pilot Art Gorbel and (left) Walter H. Beech, who later established his own company for the creation of a string of classic light transports.

RIGHT
The Boeing Model 80, first flown in 1928, was the three-engined successor to the single-engined Model 40, and could carry 12 passengers in a cabin entirely separate from the flight deck and provided with leather-upholstered seats, forced-air ventilation, individual reading lamps as well as a rest room with hot and cold running water.

aerodynamic qualities. The Model 40A had been designed as a very clean machine whose basically low drag was enhanced by the considerable attention that was paid to factors such as carefully considered detail design and features to reduce structural weight: the result was a transport aeroplane which could maintain a high average speed over long stages. With the emergence of this machine, the age of World War I aircraft and their derivatives was finally on its way out. In 1930 Boeing produced the Model 200 Monomail as the most advanced mailplane yet built. Here, for the first time in an American aeroplane, was the latest design philosophy: a circular-section fuselage of metal monocoque construction, a neatly cowled radial

engine offering good power and reliability with low fuel consumption, a cantilever low-set wing of metal stressed-skin construction, and retractable landing gear. The Monomail was a revelation, for its full use of the latest stressed-skin metal construction ensured that this thoroughly practical machine was as clean as any aeroplane of its period.

A year later Boeing produced another aeroplane based on the same core design formula but scaled up to twin-engined size and intended as a bomber. This was the B-9, the immediate predecessor of the first truly modern airliner, the Model 247, in 1932. The Model 247, which reached its most refined form as the Model 247D in 1934, was a remarkable aeroplane, and perhaps deserved to enjoy greater

commercial success than it did. Nevertheless, with this type the day of the biplane, together with wooden structures and canvas coverings was over, even though it took some considerable time more for the more reactionary aviation specialists and designers to face the fact. Powered by a pair of 550-hp (410-kW) Pratt & Whitney Wasp radial engines well faired into the wings as smooth nacelles, the Model 247 was an all-metal stressed-skin and monocoque construction, with an oval fuselage, fully enclosed cockpit and main landing gear units that retracted into the undersides of the engine nacelles. To improve the safety factor at high altitude, rubber de-icing boots were fitted to the wings and tail surfaces, and this was the first time such a system had been

used on a commercial aircraft. These boots worked quite simply: when not in use, they lay flush along the leading edges of the wings and tail surfaces; when ice started to form, the boots were inflated with compressed air and so expanded, breaking the ice away from the leading edges and allowing the slipstream to get under it and prise it away from the wing and tail surfaces. To bring the Model 247 right up to date, the Model 247D also had variable-pitch propellers, which allowed the engines' power to be used more economically. The one trouble with the aeroplane was that it was just slightly too small, its passenger capacity being a mere 10 persons at a time when the airlines were just beginning to look for something larger. However, the Model 247 did enter service with United Air Lines, formed in 1934 from Boeing Air Transport and two other companies, and did much to make this new giant airline a major force in American air transport.

Other major American airlines already in existence were Pan American Airlines, founded in 1927, and Transcontinental and Western Air otherwise known as TWA (today the letters stand for Trans World Airlines), founded in 1930 through an amalgamation of four smaller airlines. Not to be outdone by United Airlines' Model 247 fleet, TWA asked Douglas to produce a similar but superior machine. The result was the Douglas DC-1 (Douglas Commercial 1), the only example of which flew for the first time in July 1933. The performance of this 12-passenger machine was so encouraging that Douglas immediately decided that the basic design could be stretched without any difficulty to produce a 14-seater. The DC-2, as this upgraded derivative was called, went straight into

passengers at about the same speed as the DC-2 but over the longer stage length of 500 miles (805km). The DC-3 rapidly supplanted the DC-2 on the Douglas production line to meet airlines' rapidly growing volume of orders for the improved type, and by 1938 the DC-3 dominated American airline operations. By the time production ceased in 1946, about 13,000 DC-3 civil airliners and military C-47 Skytrain/R4D military transports had been built, making this the most prolific transport plane ever put into production. Even now, nearly 50 years after the type was taken out of production, there are several hundreds of the basic type still in regular service. The design was advanced for its time in 1935, and its combination of ruggedness and uncomplicated handling characteristics made it popular in the remotest areas, which are the regions where this evergreen transport is still to be found in the largest numbers.

production, and the first aeroplane emerged in May 1934. The DC-2 could carry its full passenger payload at almost 170mph (274km/h) by comparison with the Model 247's ability to carry 10 passengers at 155mph (250km/h). Just as important for airline operations, the DC-2 had a considerably greater stage length than its rival. The aeroplane also introduced features to improve passenger comfort, including a previously unknown degree of soundproofing and other amenities.

The success of the DC-2 was

immediate. By the middle of 1934 Douglas had orders for 75 examples of this new transport, clear proof that it met the needs of the world's airlines. Orders arrived from operators in several parts of the globe and even KLM, previously a staunch purchaser of Fokker aircraft, was among the first to contract for the new airliner. It was one of these DC-2s that KLM entered in the great MacRobertson race from England to Australia in 1934, winning the event on handicap.

Realizing the scale of its achievement, the Douglas design team decided to

capitalize on the basic layout of the DC-2 in the evolution of a larger machine offering better performance and payload. The result was the crucially important DC-3 that made its maiden flight during December 1935 and won immediate approval from the airlines. Essentially a scaled-up DC-2, the DC-3 was offered in its production form with a powerplant comprising a pair of 1,000-hp (746-kW) Wright Cyclone or 1,200-hp (895-kW) Pratt & Whitney Twin Wasp radial engines in place of the DC-2's 710-hp (529-kW) Cyclone engines. The DC-3 carried 21

X12214

8303-014   BETA
Northrop Aircraft Corp.

OPPOSITE

Arguably the first modern airliner, the Boeing Model 247 was the first transport that brought together features which had appeared in earlier types, these features including all-metal stressed-skin construction, a low-set cantilever wing, a cantilever tail unit, tailwheel landing gear with retractable main units, fully cowled supercharged engines driving variable-pitch propellers and providing capability for maintenance of altitude on only one engine, and fully enclosed accommodation for the crew and passengers. On the debit side, the Model 247 lacked trailing-edge flaps and was too small for the airline market that soon started to expand in route complexity and the number of passengers carried.

RIGHT

The definitive version of the Model 247 was the Model 247D with a rearward- rather than forward-sloped windscreen and trailing-edge flaps, and this view of the otherwise comfortable cabin reveals another limitation, namely the passenger of the wing carrythrough structure across the cabin, obstructing the central aisle.

The DC-3 did much to popularize air travel within the USA as a feature of everyday life. The car and the train could compete on favourable terms with the airliners of the late 1920s for these aircraft were uncomfortable and not particularly fast, but the situation changed dramatically in favour of the aeroplane with the arrival onto the scene of the DC-2 and DC-3. The new aircraft were almost as comfortable as trains, and improved stage lengths meant that only four or five stops had to be made to get right across the continent in a far shorter time than was possible by train.

While Douglas was securing the upper end of the market for airliners in the late 1930s with its DC-2 and DC-3, Lockheed was enjoying success in the middle of the airliner spectrum with its high-performance transports of lower passenger capacity. From the mid-1920s onward, Lockheed had concentrated its efforts on small, very fast aircraft of considerable range for mailplane and other long-distance operations: the classic example was the cantilever high-wing Vega with its all-wood construction, monocoque fuselage and radial piston engine, and this was produced in four-passenger Model 1, 2 and 5 variants. With the growth of civil air transport in the late 1920s, Lockheed had produced another startling design, the Model 9 Orion. This was a very advanced machine with sleek lines, mixed metal and wood construction, a cantilever low-set monoplane wing, a nicely cowled radial piston engine and retractable landing gear. A relatively small firm, Lockheed then decided to risk all it had on an advanced twin-engined airliner somewhat smaller than the Boeing and Douglas transports as it was aimed at a different market. The new machine emerged in February 1934 as the Model 10 Electra, a trim low-wing monoplane of all-metal construction, accommodation for eight passengers and a powerplant of two 450-hp Pratt & Whitney Wasp Junior radials. The aeroplane was a success, so Lockheed pressed on with the slightly smaller but faster Model 12 Electra Junior and later the definitive light transport of the period, the Model 14 Super Electra.

A low-wing monoplane with fully retractable landing gear and all-metal construction of the stressed-skin and monocoque type, the Super Electra was a delightful little aeroplane capable of maintaining an average speed of 190mph (306km/h). Its most distinctive features were the tail unit with its twin ovoid fin-and-rudder assemblies, the Lockheed trademark from the Electra onward, and the odd-looking extensions poking out from the trailing edges of the wings. These were part of the Super Electra's secret: to make the aeroplane as fast as possible, the designers had concentrated on keeping drag down to a minimum by reducing the wing area; this meant that the landing speed would be unacceptably high unless some special device could be found, and such a device was in fact available in the form of Fowler flaps. Thus the Super Electra was the first aeroplane to use such flaps. Sliding backward on tracks protruding from the trailing edges, they increased wing area at take-off for additional lift and safety at low speed; the flaps were extended farther backward and downward during landings, and thereby slowed the aeroplane while still offering lift.

Appearing in 1937, the Super Electra was in aerodynamic terms the most advanced civil aeroplane to appear before

LEFT
Larger than the Model 247, the Douglas DC-3 offered not only greater capacity but also a cabin offering greater personal space as well as an unobstructed aisle.

OPPOSITE
The flight deck of the Douglas DC-3 was well equipped by the standards of the day, and the instrument panel and controls were also well arranged for maximum utility.

World War II. It was also the first airliner to use two-speed superchargers for its engines, and the first civil aeroplane with constant-speed propellers, which helped save fuel by constantly adjusting the pitch of the propeller blades to the air speed and power output of the engine; this feature was later to become standard on all but the smallest and lightest piston-engined aircraft.

With the Douglas and Lockheed series of airliners, the USA had suddenly emerged from the aeronautical wilderness and taken a commanding lead in the field of civil aviation. Important factors in this sudden flowering were the absorption of the stressed-skin theories of Rohrbach, the fact that there was no mass of older aircraft and traditions to hold back the development of the new types, and the

ready availability of reliable radial piston engines in a number of power brackets from several well established manufacturers.

Manufacturers now forged ahead to extend the world lead they had established in commercial aircraft. With a new generation of very high-powered engines not yet available, the designers saw that the next step in performance would be with four-engined aircraft. These, it was hoped, would be able to carry more passengers at higher speeds over longer stages. Boeing already had a head start, having designed two four-engined bombers by 1935. These were the Model 294 built in prototype form as the XB-15, and the Model 299 later built in large numbers as the B-17 Flying Fortress. Up to the mid-1930s, civil

aircraft had operated at relatively low altitudes, in the region of 10,000ft (3050m) or lower. For their new airliners, the designers wanted high-altitude operation, where the use of supercharged engines would allow the transports to reach a higher maximum speed for minimum power. The problem here was comfort for the passengers for, at the altitudes of 20,000ft (6095m) and upward where such transports would be cruising, the air is both thin and cold. The planned new generation of civil transports would therefore have to be pressurized with warm air, and this presented designers with a whole set of entirely new problems. Provision of air at the right temperature and at the correct pressure was relatively straightforward, for the air could be tapped from the supercharger and warmed by the heat emitted from the engines. The main problem lay with the construction of the fuselage itself, which would have to be made airtight in order to maintain a positive pressure differential between the cabin and the outside air.

In theory it is comparatively straightforward to make a monocoque fuselage airtight, but in practice during

the mid-1930s there were considerable difficulties with the riveted construction that was standard in the period. Both the British and the French had worked on such cabins in the 1920s and early 1930s, but it was not until the Lockheed XC-35 (a much modified Model 10 Electra) flew in 1937 that the problems appeared to have been overcome. Swifter progress might have been made had the military been interested in these developments, but the air forces of the time were happy to let their crews wear thick clothes and breathe from oxygenated face masks, thus avoiding the additional weight, complexity and cost of pressurization. Such solutions were unthinkable for civil airliners, so high-altitude flight was out of the question for several years.

Douglas had decided to enter the four-engined race, but its DC-4E, which flew for the first time in June 1938, was a failure as it was too far ahead of the aeronautical state of the art in a number of its advanced systems. (This was the first large aeroplane to use a tricycle landing gear.) Boeing, with the experience of two other large four-engined aircraft to help it, developed the Model 307 from the Model 299. Using the same wing and tail unit as the bomber, the Model 307 introduced a new circular-section fuselage. Entering service in a developed form as the Model 307B Stratoliner in 1940, this transport could carry 33 passengers over long distances in the comfort of a fully pressurized cabin. Five such machines were delivered to TWA before the USA entered World War II, and these were subsequently used by the US Army Air Forces as VIP transports.

The Europeans had already placed four-engined transports in service, but realized that a new generation of

considerably more capable machines was needed for the late 1930s. They decided that high-altitude operations were an unnecessary and indeed unaffordable luxury, and therefore concentrated their efforts on highly streamlined aircraft that would have excellent range at lower altitudes. The highest an airliner could operate without some form of pressurization was about 8,000ft (2440m),

and the Germans and British each produced two interesting designs.

The German aircraft were the Focke-Wulf Fw 200 Condor designed by Kurt Tank, and the Junkers Ju 90. The Ju 90 saw little commercial use before the war, but the Condor, which first flew in 1937, made an excellent flight from Berlin to New York in 1938 and paved the way for non-stop flights between major cities on

opposite sides of the Atlantic. The war intervened before the Condor had been able to make its mark as a civil transport, and later production switched to maritime patrol and reconnaissance bomber derivatives of the baseline transport. Surviving pre-war aircraft were also used as the personal transports of the Nazi leaders.

In this period, with little need for international air transport and only

marginally more for internal air services, Soviet civil aviation had not flourished. There had been a considerable expansion in the numbers and activities of flying clubs, so a number of sporting types and trainers had been produced, but for the moment the Soviet authorities were content to let air transport develop slowly. Meanwhile, a major part of the country's aeronautical resources were concentrated

OPPOSITE
The Boeing Model 314 was the definitive transport flying boat. With the Pacific already bridged by Martin and Sikorsky flying boats operating in stages between island bases, and the main elements of the British Empire connected by Short Empire-class flying boats, the last challenge in the development of commercial air links was the North Atlantic, and it was this necessarily non-stop route that spurred the development of the Model 314 just before the outbreak of World War II.

LEFT
Boeing attempted to regain the commercial initiative from Douglas with its Model 307 Stratoliner, a four-engined type intended for long-range services and introducing, most notably, pressurized accommodation so that the aircraft could cruise above the worst of the weather conditions that would affect lower-flying aircraft and also operate at maximum fuel efficiency.

on record breaking and experimental aircraft, both of which would help keep aeronautical science up to date. Soviet designers seemed to excel in the development of long-range aircraft, the most notable of which was the Tupolev ANT-25, a graceful single-engined monoplane which its three-man crew (Gromov, Yumashev and Danelin) flew non-stop from Moscow to San Jacinto in California on 12/13 July 1937, a distance of 6,362 miles (10239km).

The USSR's more significant designer of large aircraft during this period, and virtually the only designer of civil aircraft, was Andrei Tupolev. He produced a variety of machines of which the most successful were a number of giant monoplanes, including the strange ANT-20 of 1934. This was powered by eight 900-hp inline engines, six mounted in the leading edges of the wings and the other two in a nacelle (one engine driving a tractor propeller and the other a pusher)

strut-mounted above the wing centre-section; the ANT-20's wing span was an enormous 206ft 8in (63.0m), which made the aeroplane the largest of the period. The ANT-20 carried a crew of 20 and up to 80 passengers, although it was used mostly as a mobile propaganda office, complete with a cinema in the rear fuselage, a printing press in the port wing, a photographic studio in the starboard wing, radio, and a telephone exchange. It even had generators for loudspeakers and

lights on the under-surfaces of the wings so that the aircraft could put out messages as it flew sedately over its audience. Aeroflot in 1932 was the national airline, but on the whole Soviet civil aviation before World War II was well behind that of the Western powers, both in size and technical development.

Chapter Eight

Countdown to War

The world's air forces passed through a lean and hungry period during the late 1920s and early 1930s. For the bombing theorists the most important factor to consider was invariably the weight of bombs that could be dropped on the target. Aircraft speed at first played only a small part in their thinking: there was a firm conviction that the bomber will always get through. British bombers such as the Vickers Virginia, Boulton Paul Sidestrand and Handley Page Heyford were all slow biplanes, while the American Witteman-Lewis NBL-1 was a triplane. Only in the early 1930s, therefore, did the need to combine a heavy bomb-carrying capability with high performance gain proper recognition. This led to the appearance of the first real heavy bombers in the USA: the Boeing B-9 and Martin B-10 were both advanced monoplanes of metal construction with performance equal or superior to that of contemporary biplane fighters.

Despite the currently disorganized nature of its air force and aircraft industry, France also adopted the concept of heavy bombing and produced a number of such aircraft in the late 1920s. Almost all were notable for a singular lack of streamlining and a slab-sided appearance of great ungainliness. The twin-engined Amiot

143 and Bloch M.B.200 bombers, together with the four-engined Farman F.221 bomber, were the most notable examples of this aerodynamically unrefined tendency and entered service in the early 1930s. Yet even these French machines seem modern by comparison with a British contemporary, the Handley Page Heyford, that was a large biplane with the fuselage attached to the

underside of the upper wing and the bomb load stowed in the thick centre section of the lower wing.

Meanwhile, fighters remained little more advanced in concept than World War I types. The first such machines to enter service with the RAF after World War I were the Armstrong Whitworth Siskin and the Gloster Grebe, both of which made their service debuts during

1924. Several companies produced experimental monoplane fighters during the decade, but the RAF adhered rigidly to the well proven biplane formula, usually with a radial engine, for a period of some 15 years after World War I. Later types such as the Bristol Bulldog, Gloster Gauntlet and Gloster Gladiator continued this tradition, and the only notable exception was the Hawker Fury. Powered

by a Rolls-Royce Kestrel inline piston engine, this was the first British fighter to exceed 200mph (322km/h) in level flight.

Keynotes of the design philosophy that created these fighters were the strong yet light biplane layout, the excellent manoeuvrability, and the armament of two rifle-calibre machine-guns located with their breeches within reach of the

pilot, who could thus clear the all-too-common jammed rounds. British light bombers followed the same basic formula, but carried a gunner behind the pilot and a small bomb load under the lower wings. Classic examples were the Fairey Fox, Hawker Hart and Hawker Hind. The key difference between all these aircraft and their counterparts in World War I was the widespread use of metal in the structures

of the later machines. This was Air Ministry policy after 1924, to avoid the problems encountered in World War I through shortage of suitably seasoned timber for airframes. Metal gradually became more common in other parts of British military aircraft, but as the basic design philosophy remained unaltered the aircraft were essentially wooden types rendered in metal.

Though often condemned for being behind the times in the 1920s and 1930s, the French were well up with the leaders in the field of fighters. Several advanced monoplane designs were evolved during the 1920s with heavily braced parasol or gull wings. These offered strength, relatively low drag and a good field of vision for the pilot. Unlike the British, many of whose aircraft companies had

RIGHT
Representing something of a hybrid concept that reflected the US Navy's fear that monoplane warplanes must necessarily have the higher landing speed that would preclude their use on the aircraft carriers of the day, the Grumman FF had enclosed accommodation for its crew of two and tailwheel landing gear with main units that retracted into the deeply bulged forward fuselage.

OPPOSITE
The definitive expression of the concept developed from the fighter of World War I could be found in fighters such as the Bristol Bulldog, which had an all-metal structure and a comparatively high-powered air-cooled radial engine, but was otherwise little different from the fighters that appeared late in World War I.

disappeared in the troubled times after the war, the French could rely on long-established firms such as Morane-Saulnier, Nieuport and SPAD, as well as more recent companies such as Dewoitine, Loire and Wibault. The 1920s, therefore, saw a large number of interesting fighters, and a smaller number of reconnaissance and light bomber machines, which were being offered both for the home market and also for export sale.

At the end of the decade the French air force was equipped with the parasol-winged Nieuport-Delage Ni-D.62 series, Loire/Gourdou-Leseurre GL-32 and Wibault Wib.72, all capable of a maximum speed in the order of 160mph (260km/h). In 1930, however, the French air staff realized that all its fighters were approaching obsolescence, and so issued specifications for a new standard fighter. The best response came from the Dewoitine company, which had tried its hand in the 1920s with a number of sturdy parasol types and had won a good export record. For its D.500 series

Dewoitine adopted a new layout: it was thus a cantilever low-wing monoplane powered by a closely cowled Hispano-Suiza 12Y inline piston engine (soon to become the most important French aero engine of the decade) and supported on the ground by wide-track fixed landing gear. The new fighter had a top speed of 225mph (360km/h), which was far higher than the maximum speeds of current first-line French fighters.

The USA, on the other hand, was at last beginning to emerge from the

aeronautical limbo into which it had fallen during the middle of the decade. The gradual development of the fledgling commercial airlines was partially responsible for this renaissance, but equally significant was the amalgamation of a number of small builders into a few large and increasingly well organized concerns, each operating in a large custom-built and therefore modern factory accommodating design staff, experimental workshops and production lines. Wright and Pratt & Whitney had

become the two most important and highly competitive major aero engine manufacturers, and these two companies were producing reliable air-cooled radials such as the Pratt & Whitney Wasp and its derivatives, and the Wright Whirlwind and Cyclone and their derivatives. Finally, the American long-term research programme was now producing valuable dividends in the field of structures and aerodynamics.

The fighter equipment of the two American air forces also revealed that the American aeronautical machine now possessed strength in depth. The US Army and the US Navy each had its own air force, with the US Marine Corps operating further air formations flying basically the same types of aircraft as the US Navy. Although the perpetuation of two major air forces had some drawbacks, leading to a certain unnecessary duplication of effort, the keen competition between them was a useful spur to the development of superior combat aircraft. By 1927, the US Navy had received its first two large aircraft-carriers, the *Saratoga* and *Lexington*, sisterships which could each accommodate and operate a large number of high-performance aircraft. The two ships were the first practical results of steady pressure for a naval air arm which would show itself capable of confronting land-based air power on perfectly equal terms.

Authorities in most countries with aspirations toward naval air power, principally the UK, felt that the complex requirements of carrierborne operations meant that naval aircraft had to embody a compromise between several design factors, and therefore could not be a match for land-based aircraft. The US Navy, on the other hand, realized that its

carriers would play a dominant part in any future war, principally because of the geographical isolation of the USA between the Pacific and Atlantic oceans. It was therefore crucial that the aircraft-carrier arms aircraft be capable of combating land-based aircraft. The early realization of this fact proved highly significant in America's struggle with Japan from 1941 onwards.

The most important carrierborne fighters of the US Navy were the Curtiss Hawk and Boeing F2B, each possessing a maximum speed of 155mph (250km/h), later supplanted by the Boeing F4B, which was capable of 190mph (305km/h). The US Army Air Corps fighters of the period were the Boeing PW-9 and Curtiss P-6 capable of 155 and 198mph (250 and 318km/h) respectively, later joined by the Boeing P-12 (the land plane equivalent of the F4B) and in 1933

by the Boeing P-26 Peashooter, the first American monoplane fighter, which was capable of 235mph (380km/h). Of these, only the P-26 represented an extraordinary advance on its predecessors, but they were all workmanlike aircraft notable for their sturdy construction, high manoeuvrability and generally good performance: though they had no long pedigree, therefore, they were in most respects the equals of contemporary British and French fighters.

By 1933, therefore, the design philosophies of World War I had been completely revised. There were still believers in the biplane formula, including the Italians, but this design concept's practical limits had been reached by fighters such as the Gloster Gladiator from the UK, the Fiat CR.42 from Italy and the Polikarpov I-153 from the USSR. Even before this, however, the nature and

shape of the biplane's inevitable successor had been demonstrated by the Boeing and Martin bombers, the French monoplane fighters, and the racing aircraft developed by the UK, Italy and the USA. The high-drag biplane with fixed landing gear was to be supplanted by the low-drag monoplane with retractable landing gear. This change had already begun when the process was boosted by the reappearance of Germany on the military scene.

When Adolf Hitler came to power in Germany during January 1933, he was able to order an immediate expansion and acceleration of Germany's still-clandestine rearmament. In 1935, he renounced the military terms of the Treaty of Versailles and a fully fledged Luftwaffe was unveiled overnight. This force possessed a large number of aircraft and also enjoyed the backing of a powerful aircraft industry

the fact that it also possessed failings. There were important gaps in its inventory, especially in categories such as heavy bombers, ground-attack aircraft and advanced trainers. And while the high command should have been investigating the possibility of second- and third-generation advanced combat aircraft as early as 1936, it believed that any future war would be of short duration and therefore remained loyal to its first-generation aircraft until 1940. By then it was too late to accelerate the development programme in time to make a significant difference to the air war that raged over Europe into the early summer of 1945.

Exaggerated claims for the Luftwaffe have helped to obscure the great advances made by the USSR in the late 1920s and early 1930s. After experimenting with strategic heavy bombing on the basis of aircraft such as the Tupolev ANT-6, and causing a number of aeronautical eyebrows to be raised as a result of its long-distance record-breaking aircraft, the USSR decided that the most important role for air power was tactical support of the ground forces that were believed to be the most important element of the Soviet armed forces. A new generation of tactical aircraft was developed, based on the latest advances in aeronautical techniques. The Soviets also built competitive aircraft pressing the limits of current experimental concepts so that the widest spectrum of aeronautical and structural notions could be tested in hardware form.

One of the earliest and most important results of this Soviet programme was the 1934 appearance of the Polikarpov I-16, which has the distinction of being the world's first low-

together with a large number of well planned and staffed military airfields all over the Third Reich. At first the Luftwaffe was not equipped with particularly advanced aircraft, the standard fighter and bomber being the Heinkel He 51 biplane and Junkers Ju 52/3m monoplane respectively. Knowing that military operations were still probably some way in the future, the Luftwaffe high command was satisfied with these

aircraft as operational trainers that, in the period before the advent of more advanced aircraft, could suffice as front-line machines. Newer types were already being designed or placed in production, and it was these aircraft that would provide for the establishment of the Luftwaffe as an extraordinarily potent exponent of tactical air power in the first campaigns of World War II.

The Luftwaffe was in some respects

the world's first truly modern air force: it was the first to equip its front-line units with cantilever monoplane aircraft, most of which had retractable landing gear. Lacking numbers of expensive and still serviceable obsolescent aircraft to be replaced by advanced monoplane types, the service had a head start in the introduction of modern machines. The new Luftwaffe was a highly efficient force, but this should not be allowed to disguise

OPPOSITE
One of the US Navy's last biplane fighters,
the Grumman F2F was in essence a scaled-
down and single-seat development of the FF
with an enclosed cockpit (often left open as
most pilots still preferred to feel the wind)
and retractable main landing gear units.

RIGHT
The final expression of an obsolescent
concept in day bombers was to be found in
machines such as the Fairey Fox with
enclosed accommodation and nicely spatted
main wheels.

wing cantilever monoplane fighter with retractable landing gear. The first examples of this epoch-making type also possessed another advanced feature in the form of an enclosed cockpit, but pilots did not like this enclosure and it was eliminated from later variants. The 700-hp (522-kW) radial engine was mounted in a very bluff, high-drag nose, but this notwithstanding, the I-16 could attain 280mph (450km/h), comparing very favourably with the maximum speed of 223mph (359km/h) attained by the Gloster Gauntlet which appeared in the following year. The Soviets then seemed to rest on their laurels, and the German invasion six years later found the Soviet fighter arm still equipped for the most part with later models of the I-16, and even large numbers of the I-15 bis and I-153 biplane fighters.

The country which then took the practical lead in introducing advanced combat aircraft was Germany. After lengthy evaluation, the Messerschmitt Bf 109 was selected as the Luftwaffe's primary fighter, the Dornier Do 17 and

Heinkel He 111 as its standard medium bombers, and the Junkers Ju 87 Stuka (abbreviated from Sturzkampfflugzeug, or dive-bomber) as its basic tactical support aeroplane. The last of the Luftwaffe's mainstay aircraft to appear before World War II was the Junkers Ju 88 medium bomber, which entered service in 1939. A classic aeroplane of great if not unrivalled operational versatility, the Ju 88 was originally intended as a fast medium bomber with limited dive-bombing

capability, but served with great distinction in a great variety of roles throughout World War II. In terms of versatility, the Ju 88 was rivalled only by the remarkable British de Havilland D.H.98 Mosquito.

The Germans tested the standard European concept of air power during the Spanish Civil War, which started in 1936. German aircraft were involved from the beginning, when Ju 52/3m transports were used to ferry General Francisco

Franco's Nationalist troops from Spanish Morocco into southern Spain. As a bomber, however, the Ju 52/3m proved a failure, as did the Heinkel He 51 fighter when opposed by the formidable Soviet I-15 and I-16 fighters.

As the latest German combat aircraft emerged from their production lines they were sent to Spain in small numbers for operational evaluation. It was here that most of Germany's early World War II aircraft first saw combat and pilots learned

1935. The Italian bombers, principally the Savoia-Marchetti S.M.79 tri-motor monoplane, distinguished themselves in Spain, but the CR.32 and CR.42 fighters seemed better than they were because their phenomenal agility enabled them to keep out of trouble.

The Regia Aeronautica therefore emerged from these two campaigns overestimating the operational utility of its first-line fighters. Three very promising designs for monoplane fighters, the Fiat G.50 Freccia, Macchi MC.200 Saetta and Reggiane Re.2000 Sagittario, were developed just before World War II, but the Italians had failed to keep up with the development of high-powered inline engines. All three of these potentially good fighters were therefore fitted with low-powered radials: furthermore, speed and rate of climb were also sacrificed to the pilots' expressed preference for manoeuvrability. Armament was poor, especially compared with the standards set in German fighters, which had 20-mm cannon firing explosive shells.

Like Germany, Japan came late to

how to get the best out of their aircraft. The problems with German aircraft in combat were seen and cured, and as a result the Luftwaffe was a confident and experienced air force by the start of World War II in 1939.

The Germans entered into the Spanish Civil War with a firm belief in using their aircraft in a strategic role, but soon discovered the vulnerability of their bombers when these were forced to operate without long-range fighter escort.

After the death in a 1936 flying accident of Lieutenant General Walther Wever, the Luftwaffe's first chief-of-staff and Germany's primary protagonist of strategic air power, the Germans effectively turned their backs on the concept of strategic bombing and devoted virtually their full attention to the development of tactical air power to be used as flying artillery in support of the German army's new fast-moving, hard-hitting armoured divisions. Thus the

Luftwaffe became a tactical air force in terms of its equipment, practical experience, training and operational philosophy.

The initial successes enjoyed by the Axis powers (Germany, Italy and Japan) were partially due to the fact that all three nations had gained before the outbreak of World War II. Italy had not only supported the Nationalists in Spain, but had also been able to test her forces in the conquest of Abyssinia, which began in

LEFT
As World War II approached, the monoplane warplane was almost universal, and the first-generation aircraft of this layout were about to be complemented and then supplanted by second-generation machines as epitomized by the supremely elegant de Havilland Mosquito twin-engined bomber. This was made largely of a wooden plywood/balsa/plywood sandwich material to ease demands on the light alloys required for other aircraft, and was easy to manufacture and maintain.

OPPOSITE
A first-generation monoplane that proved invaluable to the German war effort in World War II was the Junkers Ju 52/3m. Designed as the single-engined Ju 52 for the civil market, the type was then revised as the three-engined Ju 52/3m that was built in large numbers for the civil and, more importantly, military markets.

modern aviation, and developed a good air force almost right from the beginning. Although the army and navy had each possessed their own air arms since 1911, Japan only began to develop her aircraft industries and air forces in the 1930s. Content at first to build Western types under licence, and so absorb the latest production and design techniques, Japan began a major expansion of her air forces in the mid-1930s, using her own designs.

The Western nations were only too glad to condemn these Japanese aircraft as inferior copies and adaptations of Western designs. In fact they were skilfully designed to take advantage of Japan's capacity for producing lightweight structures with heavy armament, superior agility and good performance especially in speed, climb rate and range. Some inkling of Japan's success could have been gained from reports coming from China, where the Japanese had started a full-scale war in 1937, but Western intelligence staffs were amused rather than impressed by high assessments of Japanese aircraft. Yet the

Mitsubishi A5M and Nakajima Ki-27 low wing monoplane fighters had very good performance despite their retention of fixed landing gear arrangements, and the next generation of fighters was even better. The Mitsubishi A6M Reisen (zero fighter), later known as the Zeke, received a glowing assessment from Americans flying against them in China, as did the Mitsubishi G3M Nell and G4M Betty bombers. All such warnings were disregarded, and this was to cost the Allies dearly in 1941 and 1942.

By 1936 the UK and France had become thoroughly alarmed by the nature and rate of German military expansion and decided to institute major rearmament programmes in which aircraft had a high priority. France had at last divorced the air force from the army by creating an independent Armée de l'Air in 1933, but the new air force was still tragically short of modern aircraft. In 1936 the French government finally got round to nationalizing most of the aircraft industry, forming major groups in the north, centre, west, south-west and south-east of the country, and leaving only a few successful firms in private hands. The nationalized groups had produced some excellent designs by the

beginning of the war, but these were not ready for the French campaign of 1940. The main burden fell instead on aircraft designed by the few successful private firms: Dewoitine's beautiful little D.520 fighter, Morane-Saulnier's angular M.S.406 fighter, Bloch's stubby but powerful M.B.151 fighter, Bréguet's promising Bre.690 twin-engined fighter and Potez's useful Type 63 twin-engined fighter-bomber. Other excellent machines that could have played an important role had more of them been delivered in time

were the Bloch M.B.175 light bomber, the elegant Lioré-et-Olivier LeO 451 medium bomber and the useful Amiot 350 series bomber.

The British almost managed to land themselves in the same position. Only a providential blend of official demands and private enterprise supplied just enough of the right aircraft for survival in 1940. The same combination had also seen the development of several intermediate types in the early 1930s, including the technically fascinating Vickers Wellesley

bomber with the geodetic structure invented by Dr Barnes Wallis. By the middle of the decade the British aircraft industry was well on the way to producing important new fighters: the RAF abandoned the biplane formula after the Gloster Gladiator and now turned to the low-wing monoplane. The two that became best known were the Hawker Hurricane and the Supermarine Spitfire, each powered by the magnificent Rolls-Royce Merlin, a descendant of the R racing engine, and each armed with eight

rifle-calibre machine-guns. Both these interceptors had top speeds in the order of 350mph (565km/h), about 100mph (160km/h) faster than the Gladiator. With their retractable landing gear, trailing-edge flaps and enclosed cockpits, the aircraft caused problems at first in operational units, but as soon as pilots had mastered the necessary techniques the Hurricane and Spitfire won great popularity.

The British bomber force was also given completely new equipment in the shape of the Armstrong Whitworth Whitley, Handley Page Hampden and Vickers Wellington, each of these being a cantilever low-wing monoplane bomber with twin engines and retractable landing gear. There was also the Fairey Battle single-engined light bomber, which was to prove almost worthless in combat, and the twin-engined Bristol Blenheim light bomber, an advanced and speedy aeroplane for its time though somewhat flimsy and under-armed. While most of the other leading aeronautical powers had switched to heavy machine-guns and cannon for fighter armament, the British still believed in rifle-calibre weapons. To deliver the necessary weight of fire, however, British fighters had to be fitted with at least eight guns. It is still debatable as to which system of armament was the more efficient.

The Americans were producing some very advanced aircraft, including the first Boeing B-17 Flying Fortress four-engined heavy bomber in 1935, but were still behind the Europeans in the theory and practice of air warfare. American aircraft had good performance, and allowed the pilot to perform his tasks in some comfort, but they lacked the edge of their European counterparts. Nonetheless, American production was considerable, and the European powers were happy to order large quantities of such aircraft as the Curtiss P-36 and P-40 fighters, the Douglas DB-7 and Martin Maryland bombers and a number of other types. Meanwhile the Americans were hard at work on a new generation of aircraft that would make great and enduring reputations for themselves in World War II.

Thus the scene was set for the outbreak of World War II in September

1939. The war lasted until 1945 and the defeat of Germany and Japan in a ghastly war was nonetheless an extraordinary stimulus for the technical and operational growth of aviation in the widest sense of the word. The nature of the quantum leap in performance that was to be ushered was revealed when the Germans, overtaking an initial British lead, scored a considerable success in August 1939, less

than one week before the outbreak of World War II, when they flew the Heinkel He 178 prototype, which was thus the world's first jet-powered aeroplane to fly.

The Macchi MC.200 Saetta was an example of the first generation of modern monoplane warplanes, but this Italian fighter was let down by its comparatively low-powered radial engine and light armament. The type was later revised as the MC.202 with a German inverted-Vee engine and heavier armament including German cannon, and was then an excellent fighter.